Step Toward Freedom

Step Toward Freedom

Linda C. Maddox

BROADMAN PRESS
Nashville, Tennessee

© Copyright 1989 • Broadman Press
All rights reserved
4250-70

ISBN: 0-8054-5070-X
Dewey Decimal Classification: 305.2
Subject Heading: YOUTH // FREEDOM
Library of Congress Catalog Card Number: 88-8154

Printed in the United States of America

"Household of Faith," page 78: Words by Brent Lamb and John Rosasco. © 1983 by Straightway Music. International copyright secured. Gaither Copyright Management. Used by permission.

Library of Congress Cataloging-in-Publication Data

Maddox, Linda C., 1937-
    Step toward freedom / Linda C. Maddox.
        p.   cm.
    ISBN 0-8054-5070-X
    1. High school graduates—Conduct of life.   2. Liberty—Juvenile literature.   I. Title
BJ1661.M33 1989
170′ .2′0223—dc19   88-8154

To

Bob and Ben
for their literary contribution
and craftsmanship

Andy and Elizabeth
for their thoughtful involvement
and encouragement

Tina
for her gift of springtime love
as she joins our family

Introduction

On the basis of more than twenty-five years as a teacher and high school counselor, backed up by nearly thirty years as a mother, I know about the excitement of high school graduation. No other experience of commencement quite matches the thrill of this moment in your life. Even if you are not graduating this year, through this book I want to claim the privilege of looking forward to and living through these days with you.

As a counselor and mom, I would like to slide some advice, guidelines, a few "don'ts," and lots of "do's" in on you. As you leave the warm nest of home and high school, I would like to do my part to send you off with both a blessing and a celebration.

If you are like hundreds of seniors whom I have helped get to and through high school graduation, you will find some uneasiness and many questions mingled in with your joy and anticipation. Using Scripture, words from wise people, true stories of young people, and my own thoughts about this important step, I want to walk with you up on the platform, stand there while you receive your diploma, and then walk off the stage and into your next steps toward a brand-new kind of freedom.

As you take giant, leaping steps toward freedom, allow me to help you struggle with the questions we all ask: Where to? what next?

Contents

Contents

1

Free to Be

Finally, after at least twelve years of school, you have reached your first great plateau of freedom: high school graduation. For these last years you have yearned for this new level of freedom. As you walk across the stage, the platform, the football field, wherever the ceremony takes place, with all the accompanying excitement, you probably feel:

Now that I am here, no one can tell me what to do. I can take my first step into the newfound freedom! I can do and be whatever I choose.

But your next thought might just as well be:

But what is freedom? What do I do with it?

Across America, high school graduation stands out as a major springtime ritual. In schools almost hidden among city skyscrapers, in auditoriums and gymnasiums in sprawling suburban educational palaces, in football fields in Smalltown, USA, hopeful youth and proud families gather for graduation ceremonies. Such events come in a variety of shapes and styles. Usually school officials manage to maintain a good measure of dignity despite the surging feelings of the students and spectators.

In nearly twenty-five years of working with seniors and graduation ceremonies, I have seen just about everything go wrong that can: thunderstorms, power failures, no-show speakers, rowdy crowds, even a frantic rush from the ceremony to the hospital delivery room with a very pregnant senior girl. I have, also, unfailingly been moved by the bright faces, well-deserved sense of pride over the accomplishment, beaming parents, and the promise of inviting opportunities for you graduates.

I have sought to counsel high school seniors about their future with varied degrees of success. With but the rarest of exceptions, I have seen them off to their promise-laden tomorrows with blessings and optimism.

I have addressed just enough commencements to know how tough that assignment can be.

The speaker says, "You are the hope for tomorrow."
You say, "Great! I can't even get into college."
The smuggled-in beach ball sails into the air.

The speaker says, "I entrust my future to you."
You say, "Then, you are in bad shape."
Clang! Clang! goes the alarm clock hidden under one of the graduate's robe.

The speaker says, "The world is waiting for you!"
That's when you wave the MOM, HELP!-emblazoned mortarboard in the air.

The young man, dressed in the traditional black robe, white shirt, blue tie, topped off with the precariously perched mortarboard, sat on the front row of the platform waiting for his time to speak. He did not quite have the GPA to make it to the valedictorian's spot, but he had been named salutatorian, quite an achievement for a class of 390. He felt pleased that his high school career had turned out so well. Excellent grades, including high SAT scores, had gained him admission to Harvard University. Praise-worthy extracurricular activities and a good measure of public recognition had brought him personal satisfaction. He sat surrounded by friends, both students and teachers with the added plus of a strongly supportive family. But he could not deny the strange feelings, even waves of insecurity that he felt.

The speech, put together in the last few hours just prior to graduation ceremonies, frankly, to his own surprise, had almost none of the biting wit for which he had become known among the students. As he thought about this last gathering, the event which he had thought would *never* arrive, his typical cleverly sarcastic speech just did not fit. He knew that these people with whom he had bantered for twelve years would scatter to the winds after tonight. These people had been important in his life. They were friends. He wanted to say just the right words, for himself and to them, that would capture, maybe even enshrine, the moment.

As he strode to the podium for his speech, robe flapping in the wind, he saw the smiles breaking on the faces of his friends. They were ready for his delightful cynicism or, at least, bittersweet comments. Instead he said, "Look around you. Look at your friends. These are people from countries around the world. These are people of all colors, cultures, and religions. When we started school, we were a diverse group. We still are a diverse group. We will no doubt remain a diverse group. But we have learned to work together. At the beginning of our senior year we did not have so much unity. Now we have a kinship that has developed immeasurably in our senior year. We will take our 'differentness and individuality' into whatever future we carve out for ourselves." And with a few more insightful words he concluded with, "Best to each of you."

The class responded appreciatively with applause and some disbelief. His brief, sober remarks caught them off guard, yet he had spoken their sentiments.

Other speeches followed. Finally the moment came to fling their hats into the air. A happy moment! High school graduates, all. With much less dignity than that which marked their entry, the graduates surged off the football field into the gymnasium to trade in the mock diplomas presented at the ceremony for the genuine articles stacked on long tables under the basketball goals.

The night was still young. The salutatorian walked out the

double doors of the gym, diploma in hand, stopped and looked around. He had done well, worked hard. To his dismay, surprise, even irritation, a wave of loneliness swept over him. Why did he have that uneasy feeling? Why did he feel alone? His bewildering, conflicting emotions could only be described with the words, *Where to? What next?* He sensed he had made a giant step toward freedom. Freedom! What kind of freedom? What is freedom?

As a brand-new high school graduate, probably you can identify with some of the feelings that rushed through my young friend. For whatever comfort it is, you are not the first to ask these questions. Millions of young people before you have sat where you sit, have felt the same cluster of emotions, and asked the same kinds of questions. Most of them have made it, and so will you if you will pay the price to struggle with the "where to's" and "what next's." Explore your new freedom *to be.* Explore what you and God can do with your life. Stand on tiptoe with excitement and anticipate your future as you take these steps into a new freedom.

Freedom not Feardom

Ben, my son, who quite recently took the steps you are now taking, and, from whom you will hear off and on in these pages, said: "One of the first things to realize is that the word is *freedom,* not *feardom.* Count on it. You will have times that terrify you: the first college exam, the first job interview, the first time your phone gets disconnected because you and your roommates failed to pay the bill. But freedom, not feardom, will become the norm for you as you master the bumps and grinds of you new way of living.

"This passion for personal and national freedom has driven our nation since we began. Freedom is exhilarating, mysterious, frightening and, at times, exhausting yet worth the risks and hazards if managed carefully. For freedom, men and women have willingly risked everything, even their lives. For this freedom, with all its uncertainties, millions have braved oceans, wilderness, cold, heat, and hunger. For freedom people have endured ridicule, skepticism, isolation, exile, threats, and death."

To be sure, the world out there does have its fearsome aspects. You will face some tough sledding as you move into your freer life away from the fairly predictable routine of high school and home. Whereas your family provided most of the money for your existence, you will have to assume more of that load. How will you make enough money to keep up the life-style to which your parents have allowed you to become accustomed?

You have no assurance that you will find the kind of employment you desire. Listening to adult friends talk, you have heard them discuss losing jobs, working under difficult conditions, and facing the necessity of moving for the sake of the job.

What about marriage and family? Approximately half of America's marriages break up in divorce, a tragedy you might know about firsthand. The prospect of such pain for you can raise fearsome specters.

Your life will have its share of circumstances over which you have virtually no control, such as national and international issues that fundamentally affect the way you will live. We all hope that world leaders can move us toward a safer place in terms of nuclear weapons, but we have no assurance. You can work hard and save your money, but what if national policies turn the economy sour!

AIDS! Drugs! Crime!

"Wait!" you cry. "Tell me no more. I have decided to stay eighteen and in high school. That old axe of a biology teacher does not look half bad in comparison to all the uncertainties you have just described."

Of course, you cannot stop the clock. And most of you do not want to stay in high school. For all of human history, the oncoming generations have faced something of the same *feardoms* as they accepted their *freedoms.* You can also.

Let me give you a favorite Scripture verse to hang on to when times get uncertain: "God hath not given us the spirit of fear; but of power, and of love, and of a sound mind" (2 Tim. 1:7).

What an incredible time in your life you are poised to experience! Do not rest idly on your haunches and watch the world go by without you. Take it by the tail and hang on for dear life. Whether your "where to's" are which college or which fast food chain to apply to, face the adventure of youth with the zeal your young years allow. Claim the freedom from fear, the freedom to love, and the freedom that comes from a mind and spirit grounded in a living faith in God.

Free to Be a New You

As you face this time of adventure, of just beginning to skim the surface of who and what you will be, think of all the people, places, and things you would like to encounter, while at the same time, working steadily toward making some of your goals into realities.

As you claim the freedom to become a new you, you will have to, as one young person said, "think outside the lines."

Tom had grown up in the comfort of a stable, academically oriented family. His father had gained esteem as a university professor and administrator. With a solid high school record under his belt, Tom's family assumed he would go right into college, but he had different ideas. On his own he had done a bit of investigating and discovered that his good grades and working knowledge of Spanish put him in a position to teach math in an elementary school in a tiny Central American country. To his parents' shock but admiration, he announced he would go to that hard-pressed country for a year before entering college. The experience changed his life.

Louise wanted to attend a tough competitive institute of technology in another state. She could manage the entrance requirements, but the financial strain would take a heavy toll on her family. She chose the educational co-op route, making a deal with a local company that would allow her to alternate between a semester of work and a semester at college. The job would provide sufficient money to offset the extra school expenses while giving invaluable experience. It would take longer to finish, but upon college graduation, Louise would have a wealth of experience and formal training to make her highly marketable.

An especially adventurous young man decided to sign on to a cargo ship as a sailor prior to entering college. He faced stiff union hiring regulations but he managed to land a job. For several months he lived and worked among some of the roughest men, but the once-in-a-lifetime experience changed his life.

State and national governments can provide some opportunities for adventure and growth if you will look for them. Various internships, volunteer positions, and observer posts can provide the imaginative young person with a way to have fun while serving and learning.

Talk with your church and denominational leaders. They probably have some golden ways for you to invest time with people in need. The church of which my family and I are members has a summer day-camp program that ministers to children in the church and neighborhood. The ministry employs several teenagers who work under the direction of professional staff to run the day camp.

Conference and retreat centers scattered around the country employ young people as support staff. Local church associations frequently have a need for volunteer or minimum-wage youth to help operate community centers for the needy, for children, and for the homeless.

See what I mean? Think a bit outside the lines. Call up some creativity; take some chances. Now, before you have families of your own to maintain, you do well to take advantage of your unique measure of freedom to have adventures that may well elude you later.

New Directions: Friends

Ben said: "One of the most difficult transitions to make is moving on to new friendships. Friends, to whom you pledged lifelong love and loyalty the night of graduation, may recede in importance. Friends who meant a great deal to you will quietly disappear in the mists of time. Sounds impossible right now? It may happen, in all likelihood will happen between you and some of your best high school buddies.

"Just a short time ago, my friend and I sat on the hood of a rather battered 1968 Continental, nicknamed 'The Queen,' pouring out our hearts and eyes to each other. We pledged undying allegiance and a letter a week after we got settled into our colleges. I wrote him once. He wrote me back. We have hardly seen each other since that night at the old car. Does that mean high school friends are not important? No, of course not. Even now, I can remember classmates whose legacy lingers even though we have rarely seen each other since high school."

You care a great deal for these high school friends, and they feel the same way about you. Some of those young people will remain your friends forever, even though miles and years separate you. The relationships change because you change. High school graduation marks a time of new beginnings. You will venture ahead to new places and friends, not necessarily to more intimate friendships, simply to new ones.

Do not be afraid to depend on your old friends. If the friendship is built on solid bases of trust, sincerity, and honesty, with a little work, some will stay intact. You will find in the next few months and years of your adventures that allowing yourself to build and expand yourself by investing yourself in others is one of the most important steps toward freedom.

New Directions: Parents

One of the freedoms, or opportunities, is the room to be different from or to be like your parents. So many graduates come to this point in their lives angry at, frustrated with, their parents. Certainly some of you have a basis for such feelings. Regardless of previous relationships with your parents, your total well-being calls for you to move to an understanding of your parents.

You have the freedom to become what and who you want to become, regardless of your parents. That is the miracle of life, of the gospel. No one would deny the genetic ties to your family. Likewise, you are a product of your environment. But I am convinced that you have the freedom to become, under God, what you want to become. You are not fated to be a copy of anyone.

Even more important, as you graduate and take resolute steps into your new freedom, I hope you can move into that most cherished of all relationships between parents and children: friendship. Yes, you can be friends with these people, your parents. Not only can you turn to them when you need money, the car, or a new pair of tennis shoes but in time, maybe in a short time, you also can become friends. As this friendship develops, I hope you will grow to admire them more than you could have imagined while you were still a high school student. Mark Twain, as a teenager, marveled at the stupidity of his parents, only to find, when he reached twenty, that they had matured rather dramatically.

A word of caution: Just because you have graduated, freedom and friendship with your parents do not automatically burst upon you. Both you and your parents may have to change. Friendship's road must run in both directions. They must become your friends as you become theirs. You cannot do their part in building a friendship, but you can do yours. Parents may be reluctant to move from the dominant role of Mom and Dad, may hesitate to let you go for fear of losing you. You may even feel your share of uneasiness because you may not be fully ready to paddle your own canoe without them around to help with the rowing.

Years ago I heard Lofton Hudson, a Christian psychologist, say: "As long as my daughter was in high school, I did not hesitate being her father. I felt a responsibility to help her make decisions, even, sometimes, to make choices for her. As she grew older, her mother and I began to pull back, as much as we dared, to let her find her own way. When she graduated from high school, we told her, 'We have been your parents. We've thoroughly enjoyed most of those years. We'll always be Mom and Dad, but we have a strong desire to be numbered among your friends.' " As our children have grown older, Bob and I have made that same declaration to them. We want to be their friends.

Communication is the key to any relationship, especially the development of love and friendship between you and your parents. Learn to say (*Communication can be learned!*) what you want and feel without anger or a smirk. Listen to your parents as they talk with you, as they drop the reins of control while coming to know you as a person.

Carole Anne had a grand and glorious freshman year in college. She moved back home for the summer to work and take some extra classes at the local community college. During the school year, she had come and gone as she pleased, staying up late, coming in to the dorm at whatever hour she chose. She made good grades. Her parents made no effort to monitor her life as a college freshman; in fact, they had preferred not to know her schedule.

After a few days at home, she caught up on her sleep, recovered from the rigors of college life, found a job at the county courthouse, started classes at the junior college and, as she had done during the year, came and went as she chose. Her father, not at all eager to interfere with her life and certainly proud of her accomplishments that first year, did not at first comment on her late hours. But he was the kind of father who could not sleep unless he had some idea of his children's plans for the evening.

He had no desire to monitor their activities, but he rested much better if he had some clue what his youngsters were doing. He did not try to tell Carole Ann what time to come in, but the not knowing bothered him considerably.

Finally, after about two weeks of anxiety, loss of sleep, and fretting, he met his exuberant daughter one evening as she came in quite late. "Carole Anne," her father said, "we've got to have a talk. I know you did as you pleased this past year during school. Now that you are living at home for the summer, however, we have to come to some arrangement about your schedule. I do not want to tell you when to come home at night. You have summer school every morning and work every afternoon, so you will have to get some sleep. You can keep your own hours. You know that I worry when you are out late and I do not know where you are. So, I want to propose a deal. When you start to leave in the evening, give me some clue of your plans and an approximate time when you plan to get home. You can call if you see that you will be too late getting in. That way I can get some sleep."

The young woman had actually not given much thought to her schedule. Basking in the glow of freshman freedom, she simply transferred that freedom home. She readily agreed to her father's suggestions. This enabled them to make it through the summer with little hassle, a father/daughter friendship made even stronger on the basis of communication and understanding.

Obviously, I do not know your parents. But from having known hundreds of parents, I can safely say that most share Dr. Hudson's friendship dream. While you were growing up, they had to make decisions for you: what to eat, what to wear, when to go to the doctor, when to go to bed, and who you would play with. As you grew older, of necessity, you made more of your own decisions. I have to admit that, on occasions, territorial battles flared as Bob and I tried to get a fix on the changing relationship between ourselves and our teenagers. But remembering Dr. Hudson's sage advice, we made a conscious effort to get out of the way, as much as possible, to let our teenagers find their own way, so that a genuine friendship could develop between us and our children.

Maybe your house was like ours. While wanting to let you go, knowing full well you have to learn to make your own choices, your parents' love for you prompted them to keep on trying to run portions of your life.

As you move from dependency into friendship, you have to pick up more of your own load. If you want to step into freedom, especially with your parents' blessing, you must pay your share of the price. In matters of money, work, school, and help around the house, you cannot expect your parents to take your own claims for freedom seriously if you persist in the former ways of childhood.

If you want your parents to respect your revised life-style, you must respect theirs. As they try to help you get to your appointments on time, do them the favor of understanding the nature of their commitments. Do reserve the right to say to your parents, as our children have done to us: "Wait, the schedule is out of control. I miss you. Let's eat together . . . or go on a picnic . . . or sit on the porch for a few minutes." By the same token, try not to feel hemmed in when your parents say something like that to you. They want to know what is happening in your world, not to meddle, simply, as parents and friends, just to participate by knowing.

This emerging relationship from dependency to friendship never happens smoothly. In the best of relationships, the changes stir up anxieties, even animosities. Two of our children are grown, though still in the university and graduate school, and one is finishing high school, but we still have collisions. We are different people with unique points of view. Of course, we will have conflicts, but they need not be insurmountable. Sometimes haltingly, but nonetheless resolutely, we work through the tensions to restore the warm feelings of respect and friendship. I am glad to say that our children take a fair share of the initiative in keeping our relationships on track.

Does all this conversation about friendship between you and your parents seem incredibly foreign to you? No doubt it does. I do hope you and your parents will work at moving on to a new plateau in your relationship.

Interestingly enough, Jesus and His parents had to work out some aspects of their relationship. Luke, the Gospel writer, (2:41-52) described a conflict between Jesus and His parents. After a visit to the Temple for celebration, Joseph and Mary discovered their eldest son, Jesus, approximately twelve years of age, was missing. In fear they doubled back to Jerusalem to find that Jesus had engaged some of the scholars in debate on the finer points of Jewish theology. Jesus' parents, in a combination of relief and anger, chided Him for not telling them of His plans. I can imagine that courteously but emphatically Jesus gave His side of the story. The Scriptures indicate that Jesus' parents did not understand what He said and meant, but they honored His feelings. Mary, especially, had to puzzle His words in her heart. Luke concluded that sparse narrative of the teenage years of Jesus by saying He grew, physically, mentally, and in His relationships with God and people.

It is only natural for parents to want to protect you from the perils of the harsh world. If they, however, see you taking solid steps forward to reach your goals, and you enlighten them on your future plans (or lack thereof), you will see the confidence they have in you. A strong friendship can begin to develop. Believe it or not, you can be friends with these people who have reared you, who have told you no more than they have told you yes.

Emotional Roller-Coaster

In the weeks approaching and following graduation, expect bitter/sweet emotional waves to roll over you. You will not always be able to identify those feelings but try not to let those powerful mood swings throw you.

Ben recalled: "As I graduated, I felt a sense of urgency, all the time. I wanted to fit everything in. Every day seemed like the last: last school assembly, last baseball game, last weekend before summer, last party. While being eager for graduation, I also wanted to cling to every aspect of that time in my life that I possibly could."

Remember, the most exciting dimension of all these "lasts" is the incredible firsts that will soon follow: first job, first day of college, first roommate, first time everything you own is dirty and you are the one who has to do the washing.

Bottom line: Through these weeks of emotional roller-coaster riding, try to nourish your sensitivity toward family and friends, remain alive to the wonders of this time in your life while allowing the enthusiams for the future to build.

Even summer jobs will take on new meaning. Suddenly, with high school graduation behind you, your summer work takes on new importance. You are working for yourself. The money you make and save will, probably, be yours to help you get ready for school. You will need new clothes and equipment, as well as all the spending money you can get your hands on. You work, therefore, with more maturity, with a greater sense of responsibility.

Your summertime leisure may well have more maturity about it. Now that you are practically grown, toilet-papering houses and being out late with the old gang may lose some of its allure. Your exact patterns may not change as much as your attitude toward what you are doing.

I certainly wish you the very best as you graduate from high school and take this giant step into the freedom *to be*.

One day when the brand-new little Velveteen Rabbit was having a particularly stressful day because Boy did not notice him very much at all, he and the kindly, old, wise Skin Horse had a long talk while lying side by side in the nursery:

> "What is real?" the Velveteen Rabbit asked the Skin Horse. "Does it mean having things that buzz inside you and a stick-out handle?"

"Real isn't *how* you're made. It's what happens to you when a child loves you for a long, long time. Not just to play with you, but really loves you. Then you become real," replied the Skin Horse.

"Does it hurt?" asked the Rabbit.

"Sometimes," said the Skin Horse, for he was always truthful. "But when you are real, you don't mind being hurt."

"Does it happen all at once, like being wound up," he asked, "or bit by bit?"

"It doesn't happen all at once," said the Skin Horse. "It takes a long time. You become. That's why it doesn't often happen to people who break easy, or have sharp edges, or who have to be carefully kept. Generally, by the time you are real, most of your hair has been loved off and your eyes drop out and you get loose in the joints and very shabby. But these things don't matter at all because once you are real, you can't be ugly except to people who don't understand."

"I suppose you are real," said the Rabbit. And then he wished he had not said it because he thought the Skin Horse might be sensitive. But the Skin Horse only smiled.

"The Boy's Uncle made me real," he said, "but that was a great many years ago. But once you are real, you can't become unreal. It lasts for always."

Becoming real, claiming the freedom to be, loving, being loved do have their elements of risk. You can get hurt. Your "fur" will get rubbed off, even loved off, but the joy of living makes all the risk taking worthwhile.

Margery Williams, *The Velveteen Rabbit.*

2

Freedom from Ignorance

"Almighty God hath created the mind free."
—Thomas Jefferson, "Virginia Statutes on Religious Freedom"

"A mind is a terrible thing to waste." You've heard that statement countless times, no doubt. But have you ever really listened to what it says? Have you taken a minute to contemplate what it would be to come to the end of your life and realize you had wasted the most marvelous, complex, intricate mysterious machine in existence: your brain!

Stand outside and look around you. Cars zip by. Emergency vehicles clang. The wind blows through the trees. People walk by on their way somewhere. Birds chirp. Dogs bark. All in all, you see the movement, the throb of life.

What you cannot see with your unaided eye is the movement of the earth on its axis, spinning at an incredible speed in its double orbit turning once in twenty-four hours and then making its annual journey around the sun. Trained scientists can describe that dizzying movement with remarkable precision. Because day turns to night and summer becomes winter, you believe what the scientists say. You certainly experience the movement of time. But you cannot see it or touch it like you can that movement out on the street.

The increase of knowledge in today's world moves in a similar fashion. For us, in our limited way, our own knowledge expands at a rate we can see and measure. You can remember those first days of reading and writing. For most of us, the ability to read the cartoon pages in the daily newspaper marked one of life's great turning points. I can remember the excitement of learning *all* my multiplication tables. We can mark movement of that kind of knowledge growth as we grasp new facts.

What we cannot see, however, is that larger world of knowledge that expands around us just as we cannot grasp the wonder of the infinite reaches of space. Our minds tell us that space and movement extend endlessly, but we cannot see all that with our eyes. At this stage of your own journey in dealing with all this newness and knowledge, you may have learned a foreign language, caught on to some of the basic mysteries of computers, or discovered something actually worthwhile in your senior science project. At best, this is only the tip of the proverbial iceberg. In dealing with the talk about a knowledge explosion beyond your own experience, you finally have to accept what others say. Like the infinite reaches of space, we know its there, but what is happening is beyond us. Never, in the history of the human race, has knowledge expanded at such a fantastic rate. You and I live in the midst of an intellectual explosion never before known.

What's more, the expansion gives every evidence of only picking up speed. Every day someone discovers something new. We read about the new inventions that scholars and hackers put together. Some of those new gadgets, pills, equations, or machines could spring another social revolution on the world.

But enough of all this talk of the universe. You don't live on Pluto. You live in Sometown, USA. Let's talk about your freedom to move from ignorance to knowing, to live, love, study, and work on Main Street.

Your Diploma: Canoes and Keys

Your teachers, parents, church leaders, and others have talked with you about this knowledge explosion. For the most part, I would imagine, much of what they said sailed right by you. But now, with high school graduation in sight or behind you, with

that "busy street"—indeed, thousands of busy everyday streets—
beckoning, you will begin to make your own way as never before
in this mighty flow of knowledge. At the risk of confusing you
with another metaphor, look at your new life as a graduate this
way: Your diploma becomes a canoe with a paddle. When you
received that piece of paper marking you as a graduate, it was like
you received a canoe. Now, you stand poised beside a rapidly
moving river. Wade out a few feet into the stream, jump into your
new canoe, and paddle for all you're worth. A bit scary? Yes. The
river rushes, has tricky turns, even some hidden rocks, but all in
all, it's great fun, especially as you master the fine art of paddling
your own canoe.

Historians have credited some men in history with great knowledge—perhaps with knowing everything knowable during their
life-times. Men such as Socrates, Thomas Jefferson, Benjamin
Franklin, Albert Einstein, and Thomas A. Edison. But no modern
person will win that title. At best, we master only a fraction of
knowledge about today's world. With thousands of books published each year, no one person could even begin to glance at all
of them, much less read them.

Probably, unless you possess unusual intellectual gifts, you will
not learn everything about anything. Don't let that limitation put
you down. If you hope to gain a strong footing on your path
toward freedom, you will need to take a tiny slice of the huge
knowledge pie and digest it. Only as you pay the price to move
from ignorance into a measure of knowledge will you have much
hope of making a satisfactory living. What's more, if you don't
pay the price, you will miss much of the best that our country and
the world have to offer you. What I am trying to say is that with
high school graduation you take a giant step into another freedom: freedom from ignorance.

In an average life-time, scientists say we use only a small fraction of our total brain capacity. By completing your high school
career, you have made a giant step toward saving, developing,
and cultivating the bright mind with which God has endowed

you. For these twelve years you have been engaged in a struggle to free your mind from superstition, from illiteracy, from prejudice, from narrowness. Your years in school have given you some basic intellectual tools with which to tackle your world. Your diploma becomes a set of keys with which you can unlock all manner of intellectual, vocational, even spiritual doors. But you have to use the keys. Only you can insert the keys in the locks and turn the tumblers.

If you are like most of us, especially when we finished high school, you probably readily admit how much you do not know. We all have to run just to stay even because of all the new areas of knowledge that constantly break open. In every way, you should feel a sense of pride in completing your high school work, but you have just begun. If you try to rest on your high school laurels, no matter how commendable, this busy world of ours will quickly pass you. Despite the expansion of knowledge, you will have no increase personally if you do not commit to learning with enthusiasm, determination, and self-discipline.

I know, for some of you conversations about discipline falls into the same category as "take out the garbage," "make up your bed," or "get some sleep." Ben, who has certainly had more than his share of struggle with discipline, said: "Remember, discipline is striving to perform at maximum efficiency when your own interest is low. For example, you may not see how understanding logarithms or the study of current geo-political changes in Upper Mongolia help you get a job in the future. Well, they may not. But disciplining yourself to study and learn what you do not particularly enjoy or may not be your best academic area will teach you the kind of personal perseverance and determination it will take to get ahead in today's world."

With your high school diploma in hand, you are well launched into the freedom from a bondage that grips millions of youth in our world—a bondage of ignorance, of not knowing.

As a high school graduate in these last years of the twentieth century, you move out into a world with countless avenues for learning, growth, and development. You encounter fields of study today that no one ever thought of just a few years ago. For you who have an interest in math and science, exotic-sounding but essential pursuits beckon, such as alternate sources of energy and the development of super computers and super conductors. Experts who study future trends predict that undreamed-of-methods of communication will require a new range of skills, offering unbounded opportunities for those who have abilities in speaking and writing, as well as for those who can understand the nuts and bolts of incredibly technical equipment. With the world's commercial markets becoming more intertwined, a knowledge of languages, linked with training in business, could offer young people wonderful challenges.

Scientists who study the way we live indicate that the United States will become less industrialized, a process already at work that has caused some painful changes in the way people live. Perhaps you live in a part of the country once dominated by mighty steel mills. Most of those smoke-belching mills have closed or experienced dramatic reductions in production and personnel. Other nations produce the steel. Thousands of people suffer loss of jobs, forced moves, reduced income, or, worst of all, unemployment.

Automobile manufacturing remains one of this country's backbone industries, calling for a myriad of particular kinds of knowledge. Foreign manufacturers, however, daily challenge the US auto market. The heavy industrial manufacturing plants of the immediate future will require less brawn and much more brain. Begin now to paddle the canoe; try your keys in many locks.

You Call the Shots

To a great extent, you call the shots; you control your own intellectual future. Both your high school diploma and your age provide you with that new measure of freedom we have talked about. You can choose to expand and mature as you move to new levels of study, or you can allow yourself to become stifled and stagnant.

Through the years I have worked with young people who have paid the price to keep up with current events, who, at least glance at more than the sports page in the newspapers, who occasionally read a book on the current best-seller list. On the other hand, I deal with far too many adults who do not have the foggiest notion of the daily tides of events. If for no other reason than to participate responsibly in the life of the nation, you must diligently discipline yourself to keep abreast of local, state, and national events that have direct bearing on your daily life.

You will make definite progress in pushing back the barriers of ignorance and not-knowing if you will make studying a habitual process. Whether you are studying in college or studying the handbook for a new job, really apply yourself. You will find that your grasp of knowledge is directly proportional to the time committed to acquiring it.

Continued mental growth and development will give you a definite feeling of accomplishment. Remember how you felt when you walked in to take a test for which you had prepared thoroughly. A quick glance at the questions let you breathe easier because you knew you would do well, thanks to solid preparation. Only a short time ago, you spent time learning the fundamentals of math and English. Now, you build on those foundations as you move into more demanding and exciting areas of study. To be sure, if you like to think and explore to the outer limits of present-day knowledge, you will have a field day in the years ahead. We all sense, without knowing it, that these technologies, inventions, and entire fields of knowledge hitherto unknown sit "there" waiting for discovery. You could be among those new pioneers. Take off.

Some Who Made It!

Young people meet the challenges of learning at different paces, according to the rhythm of their own spirits. But persistence, hard work, support from friends, and resolute faith do pay off.

Jimmy is an example. He had a grand time in high school. Unlike his valedictorian older brother, he did not bother himself with academics too much. He played in the high school band, took part in some of the clubs, made decent grades but certainly did not fret when he failed to make the dean's list. Naturally his parents wanted him to study harder. They tried not to compare Jimmy to his older brother in their own minds and never openly said, "Why can't you be smart like Steve?" But as parents will, they pushed their younger son to get serious about school work.

In Jimmy's case, a near-fatal illness that struck his father shook him loose from the academic don't-cares. His father became ill during the last months of Jimmy's high school senior year. Something clicked in the young man's brain that said, "Get serious about learning." Later, in analyzing his new study energy, Jimmy said, "I realized from Dad's illness that life moves on. I do not have all the time in the world after all."

To everyone's amazement, he buckled down and made his best grades ever during the last months of his high school career. His parents fairly burst with pride over his accomplishments. That fall, Jimmy entered one of the universities in his state declaring geology as his major. Why in the world did he pick geology? No one knows, not even Jimmy, actually. He simply decided he liked the study of the earth and, pardon the pun, "dug in." Young Jimmy, who was unconcerned about studying and grades in high school, suddenly knocked the top out of the grades. Of course he studied, hard, with incredibly stunning results. He made the dean's list every semester of his undergraduate work, finding ready acceptance into a fine graduate school for a master's degree in geology.

Unlike Jimmy, Judd did not waste time during high school. From early in his high school career, Judd knew he wanted to study medicine. With such motivation, he could not afford to miss a beat, and he did not. He sensed that everything in high school would find its proper place in his college pursuit for acceptance into medical school. So far, he continues to speed toward his goal of an academic record that will put him in line for the study of medicine in one of the nation's outstanding institutions.

Andy's academic journey did not match either Jimmy or Judd. He made good grades in high school, even serving as state National Honor Society president, started out well in college, but let his grades drop. Always Andy had said he planned to become a lawyer. His parents warned him during the bleak days of his college doldrums that he would have a hard time getting accepted into a law school. For reasons even he does not fully understand, Andy continued to make terrible grades. After an extra year to make up for all his poor grades, he managed to graduate from college. And, true to the predictions, Andy could not find a law school that would accept him, even though he had done quite well on the law entrance examination (LSAT). What to do? He went through some difficult days. He secured a job that would provide him a living, but he found no life in the position. When Andy consulted with law school deans, they urged him to work for awhile, then reapply. When life became absolutely intolerable for Andy, he did reapply to several schools, with no apparent success. Then, as it so often happens, during one of those black nights of the soul that, fortunately, come before a new dawn, the dean of a school that had previously turned him down called. "Andy, can you be here in two days to start law school?" Could he? Of course, he could! Recently, the state of Virginia welcomed a new lawyer to its state bar association.

Lynn came from a small Mississippi town. She had hardly been out of the county, much less out of the state. The university nearly swallowed her at first. Fortunately, she had the good sense to find friends in a local church and in one of the campus student religious organizations. These friends helped her through painful bouts of homesickness and self-doubt. Lynn never had a problem with grades. Despite her rather poor high school background, she had the native ability linked with the essential amount of hard work to master any course she took. But Lynn had a severe problem.

By the beginning of her third year in college, she had completed all her basic requirements yet still had no notion what to major in. As was her typical pattern in those days, she went through great agonies of soul trying to determine what she wanted to study. She did not even let herself think of career beyond college. She had to declare a major and get on with it if she planned to graduate anytime soon.

"Lynn," a friend asked the distraught young woman, "what have you already taken that you like, better than anything else?"

"I really do not have a preference. I have not been overcome by love for any course."

After some more questioning, the friend rephrased her previous question by asking, "What courses have you taken in which you did well that did not have many female students? Maybe you could major in a field not normally pursued by women. That might be a more open field."

"Well, I was the only girl in my accounting classes. I made As in both of them which surprised the professor because I had never even had bookkeeping in high school. But, I just don't know if that's it," and tears welled up in her eyes again.

In exasperation, mixed with love, the friend said, "Lynn, look, accounting is one of the hardest courses in school. If you made As, and if you were the only girl in there, major in accounting."

For a number of years now, Lynn has taught accounting in one of the nation's great business schools. She finished her major in accounting with honors, worked for some years in a national accounting firm, then moved on to the academic world where she has served with distinction.

What's the secret of these and scores of other young people like them? In a variety of ways, they made the decision to over-come ignorance, to dream, then work out their dreams. Conse-quently, they have enjoyed considerable success in their lives.

Different Folk

Your move into knowledge and understanding will also lead you to meet and appreciate people living in America from differ-ent parts of the world. Maturity, friendship with some of the newcomers, and a grasp of their cultures will provide you with a step toward freedom in relating effectively to them. America has always received people from the rest of the world. Indeed, we exist as a land of immigrants. All but Native Americans came to these shores from somewhere else. In our earliest days, immi-grants came primarily from Western Europe, especially the Brit-ish Isles, France, Germany, and Spain. As the decades passed, distressed people from Eastern Europe poured into America, especially persecuted Jews. Then came waves of immigrants from the Far East.

One of the ironies of an immigrant culture is that the immi-grants who come in one generation frequently resent or feel threatened by those who come later. The English who settled New England in the seventeenth century despised the Irish who came in the nineteenth century. Many people have always strug-gled with some suspicion of the Jews with unseemly episodes of anti-Semitism flaring up on a far too regular basis.

In our own generation, the country has received hundreds of thousands of distressed Cubans, Koreans, Iranians, Cambodians, Vietnamese, Central Americans, and Palestinians. These new waves of immigrants pose their own set of problems to the United States. Honesty compels us to say that frustrations do mount in trying to cope with thousands of people who speak almost no English and who have little understanding of our way of life. Nonetheless, those of us who have been here for awhile have to help these newcomers find their way in American culture. Because of our national attitude toward helping the oppressed of the world, government, at all levels, pours millions of dollars into services to provide education, food, minimal health care, housing, and many other essential needs necessary for survival. Those of us who have been here awhile, who do have a working knowledge of the American system, have a large task in attempting to educate these newcomers, not only in the basics of reading and writing but also in the true meanings of citizenship.

Freedom from ignorance calls for you to understand their cultural backgrounds as a way to help them move into the mainstream of national life. You need to avoid stereotyping these people as lazy or smart, quick and dull, familiar and strange. Each of these persons is a unique individual, made in the image of God, with an entire range of hurts and hopes, dreams and frustrations.

Students across America know exactly what I am talking about. Few schools in the land have not received some young people from other parts of the world. Until recently, I worked as a high school counselor in a high school in the Washington, DC, area. In that one school we estimated we had young people from forty cultures enrolled. At one point, the school administration published the student handbook in eleven languages. Other schools across the nation have similar stories.

As you graduate from high school and move on to other pursuits, I hope you will become even more appreciative of the diversity of our culture. The wide variety of people create a grand mosaic adding an exciting cultural depth to our country.

Aspiring political and business leaders among you will have to pay special attention to the needs and desires of these newcomers to our land. Already, Korean and Japanese ways of doing business have had profound effect on American commerce. Hispanics have become a major political force. Population experts suggest that by the year 2000 we will have approximately six million people in the United States who claim Islam as their religion. Those kinds of forces cannot be ignored. Rather than resist their presence—a useless exercise since they are here—you, as present and future leaders, must come to know, as individuals, people with strange-sounding names. Learn from them while teaching them who you are and what you believe.

Flashing Lights

Freedom from ignorance means you can get smart about some aspects of twentieth-century life that can destroy you.

The problem of drugs has to be near the top of any list of current problems that can ensnare, harm, and even destroy your young life. I do not intend to give you a lecture on the hazards of drugs. You've heard those speeches. But you surely do need to enlighten yourself about the drug culture. Experts say the use of "recreational" drugs runs rampant among the nation's youth. In college, at work, and in society, you will have to make a decision about the use of drugs. Marijuana, cocaine, and other more-exotic concoctions are sold almost as easily as soft drinks.

Not long ago I became acquainted with a young contractor in his late twenties. As we talked, over a period of several weeks, he opened up his life story. He was reared in a Baptist church by Christian parents, but he began to fool around with drugs while still a young teenager. The combination of drugs, restlessness, rebellion, and, as he says, other "unknown demons" plagued him until finally his school expelled him for truancy. His deeply concerned parents tried every way to help him stabilize but to no avail.

After working for a few months at a dirty, grungy job, the teen did decide to return to high school and finish his work. Upon completing a four-year stint in the navy, he returned home and went to work. Eventually he went into business for himself.

"Recreational" drugs continued to dominate his life. He managed to convince a dedicated Christian young woman to become his wife, but still he did not have his life together. He did drift back into church, but with no serious commitments. Finally, as a result of some serious financial problems in his business that nearly cost him everything he had, he came to himself. The first order of business was to free himself, completely, from drugs— tobacco, alcohol, and the "other" stuff. With drugs out of his system, he began to think more clearly about his business problems, gradually getting them under control. Today, he and his wife are active in a local church; he has a small but thriving business, and they look forward to starting a family.

You might say, "Hey, I will sow my wild oats, and then, like that guy, settle down."

My young friend would not recommend such a course. He and his family paid a terrific price for his folly. And, whereas, his story has a happy ending, countless more do not turn out so well.

The road from ignorance to understanding also has a few other important road signs that I hope you will observe. One warns against going after fast money. The world has uncounted ways to try for the fast buck. The overwhelming majority of those schemes do not work and can get you in serious financial and legal trouble. Especially flee from any dealing in drugs. All around me I encounter young people from poor families who suddenly sport fancy new clothes, flash rolls of money, and get tickets to the high-priced rock concerts. They cannot make that kind of money working at part-time jobs. They have become victims of the lust for quick money. Unfortunately, some of them will wind up dead in one of Washington, DC's (or another city's) dark alleys or some other ugly place. Others might escape death, but ongoing scrapes with the law await them. That kind of "sportin' life" has many hazards.

No one knows where we are headed with AIDS. Opinions on the numbers infected with the virus vary widely, but we know that hundreds of thousands of young Americans will die as a result of this new plague. To tell you to abstain from sexual activity may well be like talking to the wind, but I have to. I believe the Bible and common sense teach abstinence.

Recently on a radio program aired over National Public Radio, I heard an extended interview with a young man, a homosexual, dying with AIDS. In fact, by the time you read this, he will have died if the progress of the disease stays on its normal, lethal course. The college-trained man, who, before he became ill, had a responsible job in New York, said: "I just never thought I would come down with AIDS. I never thought my life would come to this. I am totally dependent on others for all my needs. I don't know why this has happened. I guess I made a big mistake."

I hope freedom's road will lead you away from the temptation to enter into any kind of manipulative relationship, sexual or otherwise. You do not like to feel that someone has manipulated you, that another person has toyed with your feelings, your attitudes, your emotions, your life. Avoid doing that to others. Our entire culture pushes you into such debasing relationships. Most frequently that kind of unfortunate relationships takes the form of sexual experiences. World literature, the Bible, and other great religious writings have long recognized the power of sex to bless and curse. Ignoring such wise counsel, our society collectively encourages casual relationships, including sexual encounters. Movies, books, and music all gang up on us to advocate cool, detached relationships, sexual and otherwise. Freedom from ignorance gives you the opportunity to establish right relationships.

Another important road sign to observe reminds you to beware of wrong-headed friends. From your years in high school, you recognize the value of friendships. We human beings like to congregate with others like ourselves. We all have a need for friends with whom we can talk, do fun things, laugh, and cry. You have also recognized the power friends can have over you. All too often, rather than face the terror of being alone for awhile without someone to run with, teenagers associate with messed-up people who pull them in wrong directions. As difficult as it sounds, you are better off being alone from time to time than to pick up companions, male or female, whose values run counter to yours.

I hope these positive and negative suggestions can assist you as you move out into an exciting, demanding, and unrelenting world. Paul, the biblical writer, urged the young Philippian church to "press toward the mark for the prize of the high calling of God in Christ Jesus" (3:14). The prize for the high calling embraces every good pursuit in our lives. As you increasingly free yourself from ignorance, you are on a high road, indeed.

Knowledge and Judgment

While we discuss your movement from ignorance to knowledge, let me toss in another element. I hope you will do more than simply learn from books, as important as that is. I hope you will gain discernment, judgment, the ability to take the facts you gather and make sense from them.

All too often, we forget the moral and ethical limits of knowledge. I used to say, "Whatever we can think of doing, we ought to do." In that assertion I was actually lifting up the incredible possibilities of the human mind and spirit. I have changed my tune somewhat. We have mastered the technology to blow up the world, perhaps even upset the solar system, with all our nuclear weapons. Hiding in supersecret bunkers scattered around the world are bombs filled with exotic, lethal germs that could wipe out an entire county, even a state, with one explosion. We build automobiles that go faster than we can steer and manage them. We, therefore, have to act responsibly with what we learn. So, in your race to outrun ignorance, superstition, and prejudice, you face another hurdle, to make sense of what you learn to enable you to face life at it is.

Riding across the country on one of my trips with my teenage daughter, we listened to the radio constantly. I have a tendency to go into my own world of thought while driving and not listen to the words of the music, noticing only the "noise" as the car moves on. On that trip, however, I took the time to listen to the words of a couple of the songs. One grabbed my attention, the one that described the girl living upstairs, screaming because she has suffered abuse from, presumably, a parent.

The words stirred up deep sadness in me as I listened, perhaps because I have encountered far too many abused young people. Sad enough it is to hear a song about abuse, but for the young lady to expect that no one cared or heard her cries plunged me into despair.

As graduates you walk into a world of hurt and abuse, as well as wonder and excellence. You will remain in a disturbing state of ignorance if you chose only the glitter of a cheap freedom, disconnected from restraints and responsibility. Because you have both intelligence and depth, as you expand your intellectual horizons, reality will begin to dawn on you as it has not before. Like it or not, as a person maturing into adulthood, you move into a reality that includes becoming not so much your brother's keeper, as your brother's brother. What you choose to do with this rain shower of information through which you walk is one of life's basic dilemmas. But if you deny the hurt in the world, turn a deaf ear to the cries of the abused of the world, you remain in ignorance, regardless of how many facts buzz around in your head.

Open yourself to the adventure of learning. Pursue courses of study that will enable you to earn more money, as well as concepts and experiences that will enrich your soul.

Along with sports, movies, dating, and the other activities that people his age enjoy, a high school student developed a particular taste for classical music. To encourage this part of his life, his parents, who themselves had no love for the classics, nonetheless gave him a season's ticket to the symphony. An entirely new dimension of the world of joyful learning opened up to the high school senior.

Only you can take the plunge. Parents can encourage and provide funds, but you have to pay the price to get somewhere of substance.

In one of his greatest papers, Thomas Jefferson declared: "Almighty God hath made the mind free." I believe that statement. We have to approach the knowledge explosion as children of

God. As the Author of all knowledge and Creator of our wonderfully free minds, God is our Guide, and Judge in all things. We owe Him ultimate allegiance. Some of the most artful, brilliant people I know live in terms of a deep, personal faith in God. We exist, enjoy the benefits of bright minds, and a splendid world by the grace of God.

The most prized possession you have is the freedom to realize a power greater than you exists. That knowledge, that confession of faith, provides you with the ultimate freedom from ignorance. This freedom to know that power may well be the hardest to grasp. As you take your steps toward freedom, making difficult choices as you go, you will inevitably have some "dark night[s] of the soul," those times when nothing seems to stay nailed down. You will free yourself from a great burden of ignorance, if in that moment, you will bow to the Spirit of God, that power greater than you. As you humble yourself before that Spirit, you will free yourself for the adventure of work: learning, loving, living. The person who thinks he can control his destiny, is the person who lives in the blackest ignorance of all. To the contrary, as we claim freedom in the Spirit of God, we move into the wonderful light of understanding.

3

Freedom to Continue
Your Education

Youth is a great time for wishing and dreaming. Wishing is a lot of fun. We've all spent some time wishing—that we could be rich, beautiful, a famous doctor, a noted author, a Wimbledon champ, a first-draft choice. If you could have a wish come true, what would it be?

I have always made a distinction between wishing and dreaming. Wishing gives flight to our fantasies. Dreaming, on the other hand, lets us envision the possible. Dreaming, coupled with the work to give reality to the dreams, is light years away from simply sitting around wishing. You dream of earning a college degree, of having a satisfying career based on your education. Wonderful. Let's talk about making your dream come true.

Many of you have chosen to advance your dreams by continuing your education in a college, university, or technical school. I heartily commend you on your decision; it is one you will not regret. But now that you have made the decision to attend college, what next? What to expect? What about low SAT scores. "Which way do I go if I do not get accepted to the school of my choice?" "If I get into school, how do I decide which courses to take?" "Suppose I cannot stand my roommate? What if my roommate despises me or is messy or, worse, too neat?"

My daughter and I decided to drive across the southeastern part of the United States and to tour all the college campus on our route. We toured large, rambling campuses dotted with magnificent buildings set in open spaces nestled against mountains.

In huge cities we toured famous universities whose buildings were all but lost among the urban sprawl of office towers and government complexes. We likewise stopped at small community colleges whose open-door feelings gave an air of efficiency and acceptance. We drove around one school situated downtown in a dirty city. We had to pass through sturdy iron gates to reach the campus. Once inside the fence, we discovered a place of quiet solitude that made us forget the squalid, urban conditions that surrounded the school. In yet another city, we discovered such a complex of universities that we could not tell when one school left off and the other one began. We found two neighboring schools whose campuses were linked by geography but virtually nothing else. One school had a feeling of Southern charm out of the past while its neighbor institution, a military school, had the austerity of an army base. Some colleges we visited emphasized engineering, others music, some liberal arts or medicine; others were noted for their cafeteria approach to higher education.

As Elizabeth and I moved from one institution to another, she remarked several times, "How in the world would a student, who had no special ties to one or the other of the schools, ever decide?"

The choice of which school to attend nearly always proves difficult. But aren't you glad you have a choice. Indeed, the American system of higher education does give you a wide array of choices. Perhaps I can build on the information and counseling you have received from your high school by providing some guidelines and suggestions to consider as you wade through stacks of college catalogs and recruiting letters.

Which College? Look in the Mirror

As you struggle with the decision about which college to attend, you may well find it helpful to begin by looking at yourself. Take an honest look in the mirror. When you step off that platform and march out of the gate, the question "Where to, what next?" is quite individual. For the time being, everyone else must be excluded. You must decide, with the assistance of that divine mirror that God allows us to use, which way you will go. To be sure, you have asked some "ultimate" questions of yourself before: Who am I? What do I want to do with my life? But you probably have not examined your life to the degree that you will as you graduate from high school and head toward your next big step.

Think about your abilities. What do you do well? What do you really like to do? If your answer is play ball, or be in a club, keep that in mind and look for a school where intramural and extracurricular activities are important. But quickly go beyond those rather superficial standards.

Ask yourself: Do I like to be with people or alone? Do I like working with my hands, being outdoors, in charge, running the operation, and making decisions? Do I want to participate in activities that save lives, chart courses that have far-reaching impact, decide how to sell the better mousetraps that others produce, or work alone before a computer screen? An honest walk through these kinds of questions can help you decide on a college.

Now, with that mirror still before your face, describe the gifts and abilities you have. Give yourself credit for having the ability to enhance what you have, to change what you do not like, or, especially, to acquire skills that you do not now possess. Part of the wonder of this stage in your personal journey is that your life is not static. You are still growing, maturing, developing, broadening your horizons. So, do not be put down by what you see, or do not see, in that mirror. Reach for the future. But, still assess where you are, especially your basic inclinations.

Evaluate your study habits. Do you say, with so many other students, "I could make all *A*s if I studied"? That may or may not be the case, but if you do not make outstanding grades and do not have strong study skills, think twice before trying to wrangle your way into a college that prides itself on being academically competitive and difficult. Numerous students do not belong in a highly charged academic environment, yet feel compelled by circumstances to seek admission to such a school. Be realistic. Do not sell yourself short. But do attempt a realistic examination of yourself.

You may need a year at a smaller school or a different type of institution. No doubt, outside pressure from peers or parents can put the squeeze on you, but find a counselor or someone else to help assess your academics. Be optimistic but not Pollyannaish.

As you go through the loops of trying to pick colleges to which you want to apply, consider the size of the school and its community. You may prefer to study in a large, bustling city. You might prefer to attend a school located in a small town or even out in the countryside. Such choices are not right or wrong, unless you select a school that is not right for you. Try to avoid selecting a school simply because some person puts pressure on you to attend. Do your very best to make a choice right for you.

Brace for Some Bumps

Invariably, in today's high pressure, competitive academic climate, you may not gain acceptance at your first choice. What do you do?

Jeff had strong grades and a completely adequate SAT score. With high hopes he applied to his first choice. After weeks of anxious waiting, he received a letter from the admissions officer. With trembling hands Jeff opened the envelope. Disaster: Admission denied!

After the initial shock wore off, Jeff faced two options: take his second or third choice or, a long shot, ask for reconsideration at his first choice. He opted for the second alternative: He asked for reconsideration. This time, to his profound relief and the joy of his parents, he won acceptance. He has sailed right along in "his" school.

Andrea received the same notice of rejection to an engineering school. She and her high school counselor filed an appeal. No luck. The door to that particular school did not open. Andrea had to take her second choice for a year. She quickly adjusted to her disappointment and piled up a fine record in the alternate school.

You also have to adopt a realistic attitude toward finances. At best, college costs are staggering, even overwhelming. I can assure you that any young person who wants to get a college education, and who is willing to pay the price of discipline and study, can do so. You cannot necessarily attend the school of your first choice, but you can go to school. What's more, in most cases, you can find considerable financial help in getting your education. In recent years, state and national governments have recognized the importance of a trained citizenry to the well-being of the country and have made financial assistance available to broad segments of the population under a variety of plans.

Frankly, not many families have been able to prepare fully for the college education of their children. Savings can quickly run out when pitted against the high cost of education and daily living. When you arrive at the college of your choice, you will quickly discover that most of your classmates receive some form of financial aid, so you will have plenty of company as you wait in line at the school's financial aid office.

Indeed, the final choice of which college to attend may well hinge on the question of finances. Most parents are willing to make sacrifices for their children to attend college, but even noble sacrifice has its limits. Sure, dream and reach for the best, but avoid complete unreality.

You can also plan to work to help pay college expenses. I know for some teenagers *work* is a dirty, four-letter word. I am sure that is not the case with you, however. You probably have little interest in learning how I got through college, but I will tell you anyway. I worked at all sorts of odd jobs on the campus to supplement what my parents provided for me. And I had a wonderful time in the process.

Recently, I spent considerable time with a bright high school senior and his family, watching them make some tough decisions about college. The young man had achieved a commendable academic record during his high school years. He applied to and received acceptance to several fine schools including the state's highly rated university and an eastern ivy league school. Naturally, he wanted to attend the ivy league university. In putting together all the facts, however, he and his family ran into the financial barrier. He had not scored high enough to win scholarships to the school of his choice. His parents earned just enough money to put them out of the bracket where they could receive financial assistance. They would have to foot the entire bill which, for the eastern school, was quite stiff.

The young man and his parents agonized over the decision. Finally, they agreed to invest all they had and then take out personal loans in order for him to attend the prestigious university. To the young man's credit, after much thought, he decided not to ask his family to make that much of a sacrifice. With some regret, but with confidence in his final decision, he elected to attend the state university. He would certainly receive a quality education. His parents would still have to spend considerable money, but they would not have to mortgage their future in the process.

Don't forget to talk with the person who can help you the most with college finances—the financial advisor at the college or colleges of your choice. Conversation about money nearly always makes us choke, but you must face the money facts. Financial advisors have the training and information to help you find your way through the maze of the various types of assistance available.

At some point, you and your parents will have to sit down together and talk college finances. I have found that many students have only the vaguest idea about their family's financial situation. As long as the students received some of the clothes, sports equipment, concert tickets, and gas money they requested, they did not really puzzle over the family balance sheet. Most of the time, parents, out of necessity set the ground rules on money. If they do not initiate the talk about money, you may have to take the lead. Such a frank discussion can relieve considerable pressure from your parents and give you the boundaries for your own financial expectations.

If your parents talk emphatically, even harshly, about money it may well be because they are afraid. They want you to have the very best, but they have anxieties that your wants exceed their ability to pay. Rather than say, "This is what we can do," they could become quiet or angry. Let that kind of reaction serve as a clue to you to get the full picture so you can know what to expect. You might find it surprising to learn just how many parents actually call the high school counselor to say, with a note of panic in their voices, "Please steer my senior away from that expensive private school she has her heart set on. We cannot afford it, but we do not want her to learn of our tight financial situation. We can manage a less-expensive school but not *that* one."

As you think about you and money at college, on behalf of parents who agonize over the high cost of a college education, I urge you to give your folks a break. Be careful with your spending, especially on extras. Remember, they have ongoing expenses at home unrelated to what you spend. With you in school, your parents face the practical necessity of keeping up two households on one income. In our experience, we have found we could manage the basic costs without too much difficulty. What always hurt our pocketbooks severely were the unexpected extras —parties, special clothing, spring break trips, parking tickets, and so forth. Your parents want you to have a good time in college but remember the old adage "Money does not grow on trees." Be careful in your spending and you will save a great deal of grief for yourself and your parents. If you manage carefully, you will not dread to hear your parents' voices on the other end of the telephone. If you constantly overspend, you can expect some distressed, heated calls from home, and you will deserve the tongue-lashing.

Once you get settled on your new campus, the number one problem that will concern you, at least at first, is not school work but friends and social life. In that connection, close to the top of the list of difficult situations will be dealing with a roommate with whom you don't get along.

Jeanne could hardly wait to get to college. She had performed so well in high school that she won a valuable scholarship. She anticipated no severe problems academically. Her anxious but equally as excited parents moved Jeanne into the dorm, met her roommate, grabbed a quick farewell sandwich, and left their freshman daughter to the glories of her new life.

Within a few days she began calling home tearfully complaining about her roommate. They had nothing in common. On several occasions, Jeanne came in to find a young man in the room with her roommate. Jeanne kept one set of hours and her roommate quite another. Whereas Jeanne had come for study first and social life second, the roommate had the reverse perspective.

This tough situation dragged on for several weeks. At one point, Jeanne almost gave up and went home. The housing director tried to help her find another place to live, to no avail because of the lack of space. Several weekends in a row her distraught parents made the five-hour trip to provide what moral support they could. Talking with the roommate did no good at all. She did not care what Jeanne did; she did not intend to change her patterns.

Then, miracle of miracles, Jeanne's roommate became good friends with the roommate of one of Jeanne's new friends who lived in the same dormitory. After a few days of negotiating, the girls decided to do some roommate switching. Jeanne and her friend moved in together. Problem solved.

If you have a difficult roommate situation, give the situation some time to work itself out. You would certainly want to talk through the problems with the roommate. Be honest with yourself and see what you are contributing to the bad condition. Make what adjustments you can to smooth over the relationships. But if talking and accommodations between you and your roommate do not work, seek help. Discuss the situation with the resident director, the appropriate dean, or the housing director. Do not live in an environment that makes you miserable. Move.

At the time you are going through the upsetting situation, you might think you cannot confront the troublesome companion. Wade in, anyway. Talk through the problems. Then bite the bullet and arrange to move or help the roommate relocate. It happens all the time. Your college days hold too much promise for you to waste them in unhappy living conditions that could be changed.

Social life, especially clubs, fraternities, and societies may be quite important to you. On many campuses today, especially the larger universities, students find their closest friends in clubs and fraternities/sororities. Getting into the organization of your choice can prove quite difficult, even heartbreaking. We have seen some young people nearly shattered because they failed to get a bid to the club on which they had set their heart. The entire program of rush can degenerate into a cruel, almost heartless ritual. Decide how badly you want to participate in a club. Do what seems appropriate to establish ties with members so you will have a better crack at getting selecting. Then, take a deep breath. Prepare for the possibility of a severe disappointment. Tell yourself ahead of time that you will not die if you fail to gain membership in such-and-such fraternity or sorority.

Also, plan to pay a high price for membership. Heavy hazing has gone by the board at most schools, but pledging remains a time-consuming activity. Most students see their grades suffer during pledge season. Are you willing to pay that kind of price for membership in the fraternity?

You and your parents also need to discuss the financial costs for club membership. You will have to reckon with dues, parties, new clothing, trips, and all the other extras attached to membership. Do your parents understand what they will have to pay for you to have that boost to your social life?

Perhaps the greatest glory and fiercest hazard you will face is the newfound freedom that will be yours as a college student. Probably for the first time you find yourself living away from home. You set your own hours. Mom and Dad do not know when you come and go and, for the most part, do not care to know. You, and you alone, can set priorities that will guide you into a productive college experience. As you would expect, far too many young people neglect studying for all the alluring fun experiences that abound.

In most instances, your professors make no effort to keep up with you. Teachers lecture, make assignments, give examinations, and the grade "chips" fall where they may. You get exactly the grade you earn with no special considerations for your personality, campus leadership, or family ties. Most professors stand ready to offer assistance when called upon, but they have neither the time nor the inclination to single out individuals for unsolicited special help. At the larger schools, some classes can have three hundred or more students. In such an environment, professors make no effort to know their students personally. You have to decide to dig in, make the most of your time, and rely only on your own discipline and initiative.

Go for It!

I can tell you from wonderful experience that college can be the time of your life. Now that you have made the final choice, go for it. Plunge into campus life regardless of where you go. You can make wonderful friends at your nearby community college as well as at the distant university in another part of the country. You can learn as much, make a completely adequate preparation, at just about any recognized school in this land.

I can promise you something else as you move into college life: You will never be the same again. Your life has taken a significant turn. I have found high school graduation one of these pivotal corners a person turns. College is the next one down the road. Your high school memories will linger with you all the days of your life, but the flavors, impressions, directions, friends, and intellectual pursuits of college will shape you in ways you cannot possibly imagine at this point in your life.

If you are like most young people your age, you face college with a mixture of fear and excitement. You can count on confronting some tough choices once you get started. You will make some excellent decisions for which you will have no regrets. You will also make some bum choices that will cost you time, money, and pride. For what it's worth, we've all been in that same spot; most of us managed to muddle on despite those unfortunate turns we made.

Please, please, remember that you do not face college with all its bumps and grinds, joys and sorrows, alone. You have a family to back you up. You have some close friends who will sail with you. I hope you have a church that will pray for and encourage you. Even more, you have a strong Lord who eagerly makes Himself available twenty-four hours a day.

If you ask, especially if you have demonstrated a genuine desire to advance, people will help you get on with your life. I wish that I had the magic to go with each of you as you drive off to college as a student for the first time. I cannot, of course. I can recall for you the wonderful thrill, the stark terror, the looking forward and the looking backward that marked my first days as a college student. I pray for you a rich and meaningful step toward freedom as you begin that grand adventure we call higher education.

4

Freedom to Make a Living and a Life

In Shakespeare's play *As You Like It,* Orlando is about to flee from the wrath of his envious, older brother. He and his father's faithful servant, Adam, meet for what could be a final moment. In the pain of the moment of parting, Adam decides he wants to go with young Orlando, to serve him as he did the boy's father. Adam, the faithful, old servent pleads:

> . . . Let me be your servant:
> Though I look old, yet I am strong and lusty;
> ....
> I'll do the service of a younger man
> In all your business and necessities.

Orlando replies:

> O good old man, how well in thee appears
> The constant service of the antique world,
> When service sweat for duty, nor for meed!
> Thou art not for the fashion of these times,
> When none will sweat but for promotion,
> And having that, do choke their service up
> Even with the having:
> It is not so with thee.

I hate school! I've had it with school!
I've figured every angle, and there's no way I can avoid going to work full-time.

For your own, very solid reasons, you have decided not to attend college, at least for now. You have decided to seek full-time, career employment now. God made us all different. We all have our own unique needs, abilities, desires, and ambitions. If you want to go directly from graduation to work, then go. Despite considerable public pressure to attend college, you have to make your own choices. Through the years I have worked with many young people who did not like school, who had no clear motivation to attend college, who lacked the immediate financial resources, or whose family needs pushed them away from college into career. I hope you can overcome the feelings that some might try to put on you because you have elected not to enter college. You do your own thing with head high and banners waving.

One young man always had a job of some sort. He cut grass, worked in grocery stores, helped around the house, and delivered newspapers. No one ever accused him of being lazy or not motivated. He certainly never caused his family any concern; except, he never liked school. Almost from the day he started first grade, he found school a chore, a grind. His parents, highly motivated in their careers, fussed, fumed, and despaired. Most of the time they rolled with the punches. They had him tested for learning disabilities: no problems. Finally, thanks to the help of counselors and teachers, he graduated, on time, with his class.

Of course, he would go to college. It seemed the direction to take, even though he cared nothing for school. After two years with almost no academic success, he firmly told his parents he did not intend to go another day, and they agreed.

He had a passion for outdoor sports, especially hunting and fishing. When a job opened up at a coastal town in his state, he leaped on it. He likes the job, and it puts him right in the middle of the some of the best hunting and fishing land in the country. True to his past, he has worked hard at his job, made his own living, and spent his leisure hours doing what he loves best on the water or in the woods. I admire his willingness to carve out his own life according to his tastes and choices.

Through the years, I have encountered many young people who took a similar route to the outdoorsman. You have every right to choose not to attend college or some other school of advanced training.

Make Conscious Choices

I do run up some caution flags for you, however. Right off the top I urge you to *make conscious choices*. Do not simply let the desire for a snappy car or a better brand of clothing push you away from college into a job, especially one that does not call for the best from you. Far too many young people take the course of least resistance, falling into a numbing job just to earn a few dollars.

I also toot another horn. *Never, never, never* stop learning and developing your skills. Many jobs in today's market place do not require a college degree, but most positions of any fulfillment demand training. You will have to pay the price of constant retooling if you expect to advance and earn the kind of money that you desire.

Find a job that you can enjoy and look forward to performing. You might ask, "How do I find a good job that does not require at least some college training?" A good place to begin is with yourself. What do you like to do? If you could design your job, what would it be?

Perhaps you do not have a strong feeling of commitment to any field, you simply do not know what you want to do, or you are not clear about your interests and aptitudes. Find a way to take a battery of personality and aptitude tests. If you have not yet graduated, your high school counselor or career-center director can assist you in taking these tests. Beyond high school you may have to look around for an office or a center to give you these tests, but someone is available. For instance, you might try a local office of your state's employment commission. Most any private or church-related counseling center will give you the tests, though they might charge you a fee. Most of us have taken batteries of these tests to help focus more clearly on our strengths and weaknesses, strong likes and dislikes. I hope you will not wander around in a fog of not knowing as you look for a job when a few hours marking little squares on a scoring sheet could provide you with a wealth of information about yourself and get you started on the job search much more quickly.

If you have an idea of your interests or if a technician has interpreted your test scores for you and you have a direction in which you want to head, go about your search with a plan. Again, if you have not yet graduated, your local school or administrative district might provide career counseling. A person whose job it is to stay on top of local employment opportunities might have a list of places for you to apply. Fortunately, in many parts of the country, employers need good help. If you show interest and present yourself well, an employer will hire you and provide the specialized training the particular position requires.

Of course, start your job search before you graduate so you will have a position to move into as soon as you are ready. Possible employers will admire your energy and courage in seeking a job while you are still in high school. Tell them that for now you cannot go to college or you have no desire to go to college, but you do want an opportunity to prove yourself in their place of business.

You may have to move around a bit, at first, to get situated. It is not unusual for young people to change jobs rather frequently, but the young worker should avoid job jumping. We have a young friend who made a poor record in high school but did graduate. Everyone recognizes his ability, but he has not yet decided to settle down. He runs the risk of creating a terrible employment record. Not only has he changed jobs frequently, but if he gets upset at work or bumps into a better-paying job, he may not even notify his employer of his change; he just does not show up for work. Because he lives in a part of the country with almost no unemployment, he can land another job, even one

that pays a bit more, but the young man is playing a dangerous
game with his living and life.

Be a Friend to Yourself

In thinking about a career, in seeking a job, you are your best
friend and worst enemy, depending on your own attitude. You
have a good mind and some marketable skills that can persuade
an employer to give you a chance.

When you go for an interview, prepare carefully. Put your best
foot forward in the interview. You need to dress appropriately.
Wear clothes that help you look confident and professional.
Young men should wear a jacket and tie. Young women should
wear an attractive dress and compatible accessories. Prepare a
one-page resume. Think through ahead of time why you want the
job, what you can do for the organization, and why they should
hire you. Be on time for the appointment. Talk up. Shake hands
firmly. Look the interviewer in the eye. Don't chew gum or smoke
while you are with the prospective employer. Primarily use good
common sense.

Once hired, keep up your end of the bargain by coming to work
on time and putting in a full day's work for a full day's pay.
Demonstrate a willingness to apply yourself to learning the job.
Act responsibly when your supervisor places trust in you. Most
of all, claim who you are. You do not have to apologize to anyone
for not going to college. If a person at your job asks why you did
not go on to college, give a truthful answer. You do not have to
write a book about yourself, but tell the person you did not want
to go to school, you don't know where you want to go or what
you want to do, you needed to make some money, or you have
to get yourself organized before making that choice about a college education.

Avoid getting into financial situations that either tie you to a
job you do not like or that demand that you stay on the move in
order to generate more and more income. A strong temptation
for the young person is to buy a car or otherwise get in debt early

in life so that his or her job becomes a grinding means of making car payments or credit card installments. You lose your freedom when you get into such a predicament.

We've all known people who got into work they did not enjoy but hung on to the job because of the security it provided. After awhile, such work can actually prove counterproductive to you and your employer. We have known some people who went to work at eighteen or twenty-five, not for the job they could do but for the pension they could earn after three or four decades of work that held no challenge for them whatsoever.

God wants our work to provide satisfaction. Sometimes we get the idea that work is a curse. If only Adam and Eve had not made a mess of their lives in the Garden of Eden, we would not have to work. Look at the Genesis account again. As part of God's gift of creation to Adam and Eve, He gave them work to do. Work enables us to work with God in creating a better world. Work can provide us with a way to express our finest instincts. Work can bless people around us. Adam, in the excerpt from Shakespeare at the beginning of this chapter, valued his opportunity to work. He found great satisfaction in serving Orlando's father and begged for the chance to serve the younger man, even if it meant going into exile.

Admittedly, many jobs today can have a demeaning effect on people. Some jobs are so mind numbing that the person loses much of his or her self-worth. I do not believe God wants for those jobs to exist, and you certainly have the ability, creativity, and energy to find a position that more nearly matches your interests and abilities.

On the other hand, however, you have other choices. For instance, I had a friend in a small town who could find no work around his home that could pay him a decent wage. He secured a job at a defense installation several miles from his home. He chose to commute and perform a task that he did not particularly enjoy because it provided an adequate income for him and his family. Over the years, he reached the job level that entitled him to several days vacation a year. As a government employee he had numerous federal holidays. He spent much of his spare time doing community and church work. The aspects of his job he did not like were compensated by the economic and time freedom he found as a result of his work. While earning a living at a job that did not particularly turn him on, he made a wonderful life for himself and his family as a result of the job. But, and this is so important, he made the choices. Circumstances played a part, but he maintained control over his living and his life.

I recently heard a leading political leader tell the story of his grandmother making quilts. As a poor woman, she could not provide "store-bought" blankets for her children's beds in winter. Like women for centuries have done, this mother collected patches of cloth from old clothes, cotton feed sacks, bargain basements, and anywhere else. No one patch was big enough to make a quilt, but by sewing together scores of the little pieces of cloth, she could make quilts heavy and warm enough to keep her family comfortable on cold nights. Each patch played an important role in the overall quilt. The quilt would have lacked completion without all the patches.

Think of your work that way. The country needs the good work of everyone. Alone, your job might not seem like very much, but by combining hundreds of vocations, a beautiful, productive national fabric comes into being.

Make a Life

You can learn all about construction, computers, and the finer points of English poetry, but unless you extend your thinking to find meaning in what you learn, your living and life will lack completion. While some people will always be wiser than others, each of us can develop a fine sense of wisdom by taking thought to focus on the larger picture in our pursuits. Near the Oval Office during President Carter's term, someone had hung a picture. Up close, one could see buildings, farms, cars, trucks, people, and other bits and pieces of American life. Stepping back from the picture, viewing in it as a whole, the fragments blended to become a portrait of the president. Step back. How do the various fields of knowledge relate to each other. How best for you to make life better for yourself and others as you discover how those tiny micro chips work. Discover not only what Robert E. Lee did as a great general, but why he did it. What made him great? What can you learn from people like him that can enrich your own experience?

Whether you attend college, or for that matter, another day of school, I hope you will decide that your life will have depth and breadth. Believe me, I have seen people with several degrees attached to their names make a terrible mess out of their lives and those around them. I have also seen men and women who had not gone through college become esteemed members of their communities and churches, living exemplary lives. What you do with your life is really up to you and all that finally matters to you and God.

During a teaching and counseling career of twenty-five years, I have helped hundreds of young people get to and through high school graduation. They have adopted a wide variety of personal approaches to life, such as:

Live and let live.

Eat, drink, and be merry.

I'm OK, you're OK.

We can change the world.

Down with tradition.

Money is my goal.

Power is the stuff of life.

This is *my* time.

For me to live is Christ.

No doubt you will have brushes with several of these life-styles as you go along. These days right after graduation, by choice and circumstances, will nudge you to struggle with yourself, to discover more clearly what kind of person lives in your skin. The path toward freedom has a firmer foundation if you will puzzle over what is happening to you in this post-graduation process. Try to take a step back every now and then to get a fix on what you are doing, saying, and becoming as you emerge from the relatively warm nest of high school.

As you think about making a living and a life, I want to suggest two words to you: *unlocking* and *courage*. At first they may seem unrelated to each other. I believe, however, the two concepts can go a long way toward helping you find fulfilling work as well as significance in your life.

Unlocking is the power we possess to open ourselves to work, new areas of experience, unexplored feelings, invigorating friends, and so on. Unlocking relates to claiming the freedom to be, to overcome ignorance, to find the right school to attend, finally, to every area of life. Unlocking has its unnerving aspects because we have to do it for ourselves. Ultimately no one can do the unlocking for us.

At this point of taking the risk to do some unlocking, courage comes into play. We have to exercise courage to unlock the new and go into strange places in the world or in our own minds.

I have a young friend who has undeniable abilities. He has strong convictions, definite ideas, and a neat appearance. He does have a hang-up: He has a terrible time looking for a job. Fear of rejection, a measure of insecurity, and an unfounded but nonetheless real lack of confidence combine to inhibit him in a job search. That is until recently.

He was home for the summer, and he had to have a job. One turned up in an office doing work that he despised. For several days he agonized. He understood his utter distaste for job hunting, but he also recognized that this present position would take a fierce toll on his outlook on life. He knew not to quit his present job until he found a new one. Finally, calling up every ounce of courage he could muster, he began making "cold" calls to firms where he might find work. Pay dirt. After just a few calls, he secured an interview, met his prospective employer, and immediately landed an ideal job. You see, he unlocked new doors in his own mind, called up inner courage, and crossed an important threshold. Not only did he get a terrific job but also he found something brand-new in his own spirit.

Amy Carter, daughter of former President Jimmy Carter, has gone through many attitudes about her own life since she finished high school a few years ago. I believe Amy has called on courage to help her unlock some mental and spiritual doors. She has had her struggles academically, and she has not always given evidence of clear fix on her immediate goals. Amy has, however, consistently demonstrated that she has decided not simply to float along basking in the shadow of her parents' considerable celebrity. She has taken a stand for her convictions. Some journalists have caricatured Amy as a throw back to the hippies of the 1960s, a leftover rebel, a crusader. Yet, as I look at her, especially when I realize the easy life she could enjoy, her courage sparks me all the more. I have the strongest belief that she will do well academically and that she will make a distinct difference with her life as she unlocks more of her life and acts courageously on the strength of her beliefs.

I encountered the story of a gifted, young architect who happened to be black. He struggled hard to break into the world of design and construction, to unlock those massive professional doors. His big break came with the offer of a commission to develop a large shopping center. He moved headlong into the project until he discovered that much of the funding for the enterprise came either directly or indirectly from South Africa. He tried, desperately, to persuade the developers to seek other sources of money. When they finally refused, he declined the contract. He made a tough, tough decision that took every ounce of moral courage he could find. His choice cost him part of his living, but immeasurably enhanced his life.

If you move into a career that allows you both good income and fulfilling work, great. I have known many young people, however, who chose careers which offered personal satisfaction but less money.

One of my most talented classmates in college chose to side- step a lucrative career in sales and business to enter teaching and coaching. Almost thirty years later, he still has to watch his dimes and dollars to make ends meet, but he has touched the lives of thousands of young people during his distinguished career as an educator.

Jason recently finished near the top of his law school class, winning a prestigious special award for his contribution to the study of law. Big-name law firms from around the country made him handsome offers. He decided to join a smaller firm that had a commitment to doing public service law. The young lawyer will certainly have adequate, though not lavish, income, but he draws greater satisfaction from his work representing causes and people who need top-notch legal representation but who cannot afford the normal fees.

When one young couple married, they both labored away at their jobs and enjoyed their lives together. They promised themselves that when they had children, the wife would stay home with the youngsters and the family would make the necessary financial adjustments. Sure enough, when children came, she left her job and stayed home to give their children the kind of start in life that Mom and Dad wanted them to have. The family had less material things, but they drew profound satisfaction from the way they lived their lives.

At a special point in our lives, my family and I met the late comedian John Belushi. At a party we attended, he and Dan Akroyd, his sidekick, came bounding into the room. They jumped and cavorted around for a few minutes, then John dropped down in a chair beside my husband and me. When he learned that we were in religious work, John said, "I grew up going to church. My folks took me to church all the time. When I got grown, I stopped going." Then, it seemed as though he caught himself about to reveal something of his true self. He jumped up from the chair, resumed his crazy antics, and quickly pranced out the door. We never saw him again but shook our heads in sadness several years later when he died such a tragic and unnecessary death. John Belushi had great skills at making a living, but, apparently, he knew little about making a life.

By contrast, while on a trip to Thailand with Rosalynn Carter in 1979, Bob, my husband, met a young man named Buddy Johnson in one of the Cambodian refugee camps. "What do you do here, Buddy?" Bob asked the twenty-year-old American.

"My parents are CMA missionaries to Thailand. I speak the language fluently. I also like to build. I have a team of Thais, and we have put up this hospital shelter. One thousand refugees can gather under this makeshift cover to get out of the burning sun and receive some medical treatment."

When asked why he chose to invest his life in Thailand rather than returning to America where he could enjoy campus life as a student, Buddy declared quickly, "This is where I need to be. This is where God wants me, for now." Then with a wave of his hand, he jumped into his jeep and headed toward another campsite that needed hospital and cooking shelters constructed.

Buddy Johnson chose to emphasize making a life over making a living.

Fortunately, in America, most of you can decide to make both a living and a life. Hear the words, "Life is not to be simply equated with the abundance of things one possesses." (See Luke 12:23.) You owe it to yourself to make a life, as well as a living, for yourself and for your present and future family.

You could, perhaps, look at making a living and a life this way: Become involved. Take a chance. Touch and be touched.

WHAT COLOR IS LOVE?

> Here's my hand, don't take a look at it,
> For if you look at it, you may not see
> The kind of man you'd like a friend to be,
> Who may live inside of me.
> What color is courage, what color loyalty?
> What color is truth?
> What color is love?

Here's my hand, don't take a look at it,
For if you look at it you'll never know
How many times I've had to fight with it,
Or wipe a tear with it, that doesn't show.
What color is heartache, what color loneliness,
What color is hate?
What color is love?

What color is life, what is our destiny?
What color is hope, what will the future be?
What color is love, when will you make a start?
Close your eyes and open up your heart.

Here's my hand, don't take a look at it,
Just put your hand in it, together we
Can walk this land and show the whole wide world
That we can live in harmony.
What color is love, just close your eyes and see.
What color is love, here's how it ought to be.
The color of love is the color of you and me.

And so, young people of the twenty-first century, whatever you do with the rest of your lives, be the best!

Eleanor Wright, "What Color Is Love?" Used by permission.

5

Freedom to Contribute

Closely tied to making a life and a living is the freedom to contribute to friends, family, church, and to our land.

I grew up under the watchful eye and quick wits of a mother who had a proverb, an adage, or a Scripture for every situation. When I think of your freedom to contribute to the world around you, two of those sayings come to mind: "If you want your song to endure, write it on the hearts of men," and "You only keep what you give away."

I suppose the older generation always has a tendency to regard the younger crowd as selfish, looking out primarily for number one. Your generation has picked up the unpleasant nick name of the "me generation." I hope that tag does not belong on you, but I would like to give you a nudge in the direction of thinking about your contributions that can make a genuine difference in the world.

I hope you can realize the value of your contributions. You have energy, spirit, the courage of your convictions, unbounded optimism, and the will to work for what you believe in. You have not become jaded by disappointments, as some adults have. The older people around you need the specific contributions you can make. Equally as much, however, we need to feel and see your willingness to pick up where we have left off. Those of us who have been around for awhile take heart just from seeing the steady determination with which you set about to clean up our mistakes, build on the foundations we have laid, and explore worlds we did not know about or were afraid to penetrate.

Do not give into the temptation that would stifle your efforts by making you doubt your abilities. You might be tempted to say: "Look, I'm only eighteen. What can I do?"

The Bible has a word for you at that point: Do not look down upon your youth. (See 1 Tim. 4:12.) Don't you dare make light of your young years. What's more, don't you dare let anyone else make fun of you simply because your birthday cake is not covered with candles. Time, education, or finances might impose some limits, but you can make your mark now and begin preparing for even greater contributions in the future.

Decide to Contribute

As with the other directions we have talked about in these pages, the step toward making contributions requires a decision. Along the way you decide you will devote part of your time, thought, money, and commitments to making life better for others. For some people, the decision to become involved with others comes quite easily. Their temperament lends itself to reaching out to people and situations that need extra attention.

For most of us, however, contributing to others does not flow quite as easily. We have a natural tendency to concentrate on ourselves. Sometimes we get the idea that we should wake up in the morning feeling warm and fuzzy about feeding the hungry, housing the homeless, visiting the sick, or giving money to help the underprivileged in remote corners of the world. Not so. Maybe for Mother Teresa in India, but not for most people. Personally, I do not feel embarrassed to admit that I make decisions to contribute. Remember Ben's word earlier in the book about discipline? You might want to look back at Chapter 2 to refresh yourself. "Discipline is striving to perform at maximum efficiency when your own interest is low." Just as you decide to discipline yourself to work and study, you discipline yourself to act on your decisions to make a contribution.

A friend of ours bought a brand-new station wagon, the prettiest, shiniest car in town, or so he thought. Shortly after buying the car, he parked it on the street in front of his house in a small, south Georgia town. An elderly lady walked by, started chatting with my friend and noticed his fancy car. "What a pretty car," she remarked. "How does that back end open up?

He proudly showed her the buttons and latches that allowed the tail gate to open giving easy access to the large open space inside the station wagon.

"My cousin out in the country has a load of firewood she will give me, if I can get it hauled into town. Could you take me out to her place and help me get that wood to my house before it gets too cold?" she asked openly and innocently.

My friend, normally a rather caring person, gulped, quickly imagined how messy his beautiful car would look cluttered with firewood, and made a lame excuse for not assisting the elderly lady. He quickly slipped away from her while she stood on the sidewalk talking with my friend's wife.

Years later, he still remembers, with regret, his unwillingness to make the car available to a person in obvious need. In just a short time, the rear end of the car became dirty and cluttered anyway. For the guilt he has carried he could have put his elderly neighbor in his fancy car, driven out in the country, brought in the wood, and enjoyed her admiration forever. He made an unfortunate decision not to come to the assistance of one of God's children who had a need he could have easily met.

Contribution and Responsibility

Another important aspect of our freedom to contribute is a sense of responsibility. As a young person with many talents, I hope you will *develop* a sense of responsibility to your world and its people. Everyday you rub shoulders with people who have considerable abilities. They make good grades, show promise of doing well in college and of going on to make an adequate living for themselves. The problem is that far too many show little sense of responsibility; they demonstrate only a meager willingness to look beyond themselves. In recent survey of graduating high school seniors the young people were asked what they most wanted out of life. The majority answered, "I want to make lots of money." Most of us have that desire. I hope, however, you will not allow making money to overshadow a service motivation in your life. Decide that, indeed, you will earn all the money you can, but decide, also, that you will invest yourself in something worthwhile outside yourself. Decide to develop a sense of responsibility.

Regardless of how you might feel about the politics of the famous American Kennedys, their biographies reveal that their parents and grandparents drilled into the children the responsibility for community service. Wealth and privilege gave the Kennedys no license simply to drift along living only a life of indulgence. That remarkable family, stalked by tragedy, has accumulated a notable record for public service.

OK, you say. When I finish college, get some money in the bank, own my home, and have my car paid for, I will look around for something good to do for someone.

I hope you will not wait that long. Open your eyes now to the needs of others. A part of your world needs you now. In reality, if you wait until you have all those tasks behind you, you may become so disillusioned, so worn out, maybe even so absorbed in yourself, that you will have lost the ability to give others a second thought. Right now, you lay the foundations for the future course of your own life, which brings me to another point.

Everyday, just as you meet people with positive if somewhat selfish motivations, you also rub shoulders with people who are making self-destructive decisions. You encounter young people, maybe even friends, who want you to participate in activities that compromise your standards, that could even cost you your life. What is your responsibility to yourself, to your peers, in such instances? Now that you have graduated and moved into a new dimensions of freedom, where do you draw the line between having fun and doing damage to yourself and others? How do you avoid guilt when your personal, carefully considered choices do not match those of your parents? What responsibilities do you have to your parents and others as opposed to yourself? Is it true that you are only young once and that this responsibility "jag" is a bit much at this time in life?

Some adults, parents, and teachers tell you that there is only one way to go: their way. Others will say anything goes. Without getting into an argument, I say there is usually a *best* decision for us in a given situation though we certainly do not always make that preferred choice. All of us have chosen an act that goes against the philosophy and ideals of our parents, our church leaders, and even our own best interests. Most of you will make a choice that causes you some guilt and measure of remorse. What then is your responsibility? What kind of contributions can you make in such tough situations?

You have a responsibility to yourself to evaluate carefully your world and your choices. If you become crippled by bad decisions, you will make few contributions to others. During these days of youth, you have your best opportunity to decide to live life to its fullest. Take advantage of these days to engage in your own exploration and growth. While I do not expect you to become serious and philosophical at eighteen neither can you disregard your responsibilities. Claim the freedom to act responsibly.

What then can you contribute? No, I am not going to swamp you with suggestions, but I would like to spark your imagination.

Contribution to Friends

As you decide to act responsibly toward others, especially your friends, you become positioned to make a substantial contribution to them. You can make a difference in their lives both for now and the future.

On the other hand, if you succumb to the pressure of taking the easy way out, turning your back on the seriousness and consequences of drug abuse, vandalism, sexual activity, or other such problems, you undercut your own values and run the risk of hurting some of your best friends. You lose all the way around. Invariably, when we try to outrun our basic responsibilities, our actions come back to haunt us. When we allow basic moral systems to erode, we all suffer.

Your student generation may well face the toughest moral challenge in history. You inherited part of your problems from a previous generation. As you have studied recent history, you have read about the youth rebellions of the 1960s. In many ways, the effects of the rebellion of the 1960s have come to rest on the shoulders of the graduates of the present day.

During the days of the 1960s, millions of American youth rebelled against the status quo, against what they regarded as injustice and inhumanity. Students marched, protested, wrote political pamphlets, and even went to jail as an unmistakable way to trumpet their deep concerns.

Though I am not a "sixties child," I can identify with some of the feelings of that era. I applaud the positive changes that emerged from those efforts. However, the nation has experienced considerable negative fallout. In an effort to open the country to positive changes in the area of human relations and social responsibility, important ethical boundaries became blurred, even disregarded, especially in the areas of drug abuse and sexual activity. Society always faces the danger of pushing the pendulum too far as it takes strides to right wrongs and alter deeply entrenched directions. That negative fallout poses problems for your generation. The pendulum has swung too far; however, I believe we are seeing the beginnings of the restoration of balance.

Because of the lifting of some sexual taboos in the sixties, our country wrestles with an unhealthy sexual license. Every year, hundreds of thousands of young people go too far sexually and suffer physical and emotional wounds that can prove difficult to overcome. The country struggles with the terrible problem of teenage pregnancy that results in an unconscionable number of abortions or thousands of babies born, literally to children ill prepared to offer much as parents.

Adults in the home, church, and community have a major role to play in promoting sexual responsibility, but the most effective teachers are youth themselves. Some genuine progress can be made if you:

- adopt the biblical standard of waiting for marriage to enjoy sex
- will make it popular to avoid premarital sex
- help create a climate in which young people can have a good time without becoming heavily involved sexually.

Try as they might, parents cannot monitor all your activities. With automobiles so readily available, with parents working weird schedules creating long spans of time when their teenagers have no supervision, irresponsible sexual activity can wreak havoc. What's more, far too many adults carry on sexual affairs themselves, providing poor role models.

Thus, as you accept responsibility for your own moral behavior and are willing to help your peers understand themselves, you can make a distinct contribution to your friends. More directly, you can work in programs and centers in your community that address youth problems. Various drug rehabilitation programs cry for volunteers who will work with their fellow distressed teenagers. Local chapters of Students Against Drunk Drivers (SADD) provide young people with a support group to take the glamor off drinking and driving.

The miracle of God in our lives is that we remain, forever, open to the possibility for growth and change. But the older we get, the more difficult it is for us to make major course changes. Chart your course now, while your mind and spirit have such splendid bounce.

Contribution to Family

The family stands out as the oldest institution on the earth. From the beginning of the human race, men and women have lived in some sort of family arrangement. Families succeed or fail in terms of the willingness of their members to contribute. In years past, the very survival of the family depended on the ability of individual members to hunt, fish, farm, and provide clothing and shelter. With no government "safety net" for hard times, families lived or died by their wits and hard work.

In our day, especially in the United States, family life has changed. Only a few decades ago, the American family consisted of a mother, father, and children. They all had the same last name. The father provided income for the family while the mother stayed home and managed the family. You know from your own experience how completely different the makeup of the family has become. Divorce has struck millions of families creating step families, yours-mine-and-ours children, nearly always accompanied by profound stress. Even in homes where divorce and stepfamilies have not entered the picture, family relationships have changed. In a majority of families, husband and wife work outside the home.

Parents do most of the work to provide food, clothing, and shelter, as well as the extras of life. Though I have worked with some teenagers whose families absolutely depended on their income, generally speaking, family survival does not depend on children and youth working shoulder to shoulder with Mom and Dad. In most homes, young people have responsibilities, but they are more in the nature of chores: take out the garbage, clean up the house, cut the grass, baby sit younger brothers and sisters, run errands, and so forth.

If your family does not depend on your labor to put food on the table, what then can you contribute to the family? Many young people work to provide their own clothes, gasoline, and spending money. Some go to work so they can afford a car and insurance. In a few instances, I have encountered young entrepreneurs who learned how to make money. By the time they finished high school, they had put aside in the bank rather hefty sums.

Most of the time, however, American teenagers contribute to the family's life in ways other than financially. A general attitude of helpfulness, being part of the family, and remaining sensitive to the impact of your actions on the entire family go a long way toward making a difference on those closest to you. I hope you will work on an attitude, if it exists, that would lead you to believe the rest of the family owes you special treatment. No one expects you to like everything that goes on in your family. After all, you have feelings, needs, ambitions, and desires that may run counter to that of your parents and other family members. You will make a genuine contribution to your family if you will make a conscious effort to balance your own interests with the rest of the family. What do I mean?

Money, for instance. Most every family I know about has some trouble with finances. Even those who have a great deal of money engage in debates—sometimes heated—about how to spend their money. Your family probably does not have unlimited money so your parents have to decide how to allocate what they have. You can make a distinct contribution to the family if you will try to see the larger financial picture. Earn what money you can; give your parents as much warning as possible about upcoming events and needs that take extra money. You will help out the family's finances if you will curtail your requests for such items as fancy clothes, expensive entertainment, automobiles, and so forth. If you have a need to take a date to an expensive restaurant and show, plan ahead; earn the money yourself. Don't get bent out of shape if your parents say, "Sorry, we just do not have the money to do that right now."

Now that you have finished high school, another way you can make a contribution is to assume a greater measure of leadership for younger members of your family, both brothers and sisters as well as cousins. Children and younger teenagers regard you as fully grown, able to leap tall buildings in a single bound, with all the answers. Avoid arrogance, but exert a healthy leadership role on those behind you. Set a solid example. Be fair to younger members of the family. Around our house, I have always appreciated the way our older son enjoyed going places with his younger brother and sister. That same attitude carried over to our second son in relationship to our youngest child, a daughter. The net effect is that they are all quite close and enjoy time with one another, even though they have different interests.

While writing this book, my mother became ill, and I had to travel to another state for over two weeks. I had a business to run, the book to complete, a house to maintain, and other responsibilities. My family pitched in to help me during that tough time. We had to talk on the phone often to keep everything reasonably manageable, but we made it. The time with my mother would have proven even more stressful if the children and my husband had not done so much to take up the slack. Through the years, I have seen other young people go way beyond themselves in bridging gaps in the family during hard times. I have also seen some teenagers grow angry, resentful, and quite petty during family emergencies. Your willingness to roll with the punches in those hard times can make a big difference in the family's ability to cope and emerge as winners.

In time, most of you will create your own family. You will contribute a new link in this saga of humanity. Make a good "ready" for that exciting time. Do not be afraid to make a commitment to a person, to expect to have one mate, for life. Do not be afraid to risk yourself with another person. Love is good, and it *is* all that it is cracked up to be. When you contribute a family unit, a love match, if you please, you honor God, do yourself a wonderful favor, and make a substantial gift to our country and to the future.

Looking for *that* special person can prove frustrating. College and career young people sometimes get fearful that acceptable candidates for marriage partners might be running out. These people can fall into the temptation to grab anyone just to have someone to love. Do not rush into a serious relationship. Your friends at work or church might think that you and "whoever" just belong together. You alone know. Listen to your own inner drummer.

In a recent television movie, a young teenager explained the boy/girl relationships to his friends saying, "We don't date anymore. That's old fashioned. We just meet and go to bed together." Unfortunately that might be true for some people. But if you are following biblical standards and really want to form the right kind of relationship, if you really want to love a person and build a life together, you have the right and responsibility to get to know that person in a dating relationship. Dating is good. This is certainly not a book on dating, but a large part of your freedom hinges on this aspect of your life. You cannot imagine the bondage that can grip you if you build love and marriage on the wrong foundation. I assure you from many years of experience that marriage and family life can be rewarding and fulfilling when it is built on a solid foundation. Hang on to your patience. The Lord and your best judgment will lead you to the right person.

Two young people had finished college in the early 1980s, moved to an area many miles from where they graduated, and gone to work. Both had gone through rather trying relationships with other people that left them wary of falling in love again. They knew they wanted to meet someone to love and marry, but the wounds of those previous relationships still smarted and made them quite cautious.

In true, storybook fashion, another couple, Andy and Tina met at church. She taught Elizabeth, Andy's sister, in Sunday School. He came home from graduate school at Christmas, met Tina through his sister, and asked her out for a date.

Within a few weeks, she arranged to journey to his campus as part of a business trip. They began to talk in earnest. Soon, these two young people had fallen quite hard for each other. By Easter break, they knew something quite special existed between them. They took some extra time during the July 4 holiday to travel to her hometown to meet her family. By the end of that summer, she wore his engagement ring, and they had set their faces and hearts on a June wedding the following year, immediately upon his graduation from law school.

Andy and Tina tell all who will listen, "Wait. Do not get hasty. In God's own good time, the right person for you will come along. Until that time, have a good time, get to know people, but do not overcommit yourself. The right one certainly makes the waiting worthwhile."

Perhaps the words of this Christian song can help us get a clearer fix on the wonders of family and the contribution we can make to that oldest, most basic part of our world.

HOUSEHOLD of FAITH

Here we are at the start, committing to each other
By His word and from our hearts.
We will be a family in a house that will be a home,
And with faith we'll build it strong.

We'll build a household of faith that together we can make.
And when the strong winds blow it won't fall down.
As one in Him we'll grow and the whole world will know
We are a household of faith.

Now, to be a family, we've got to love each other
At any cost, unselfishly.
And our home must be a place that fully abounds with grace,
A reflection of His face.

We'll build a household of faith that together we can make.
And when the strong winds blow it won't fall down.
As one in Him we'll grow and the whole world will know
We are a household of faith.

Church

I hope you take an active part in a church near where you live. If you do not, I encourage you to look around and find a faith community in which you can participate. You will find your life more manageable as you move in a circle of friends with a genuine and growing faith in God.

For most of you who read this book, I make the assumption that you do participate in a church of one denomination or another. Your local church, or one in your part of the community, provides numerous ways for you to contribute, especially now that you have reached the mark of high school graduation or near graduation. Talk with the minister or a member of the church staff. Help him or her decide what abilities or interests you have and how best to use the innate gifts you possess. You can work with younger children in church school, day camp, day care, mothers' day out programs, or choirs. Most every church I know about has a chronic shortage of people who will help.

Depending on your location, you can find numerous other avenues of service through the various churches. Community centers, shelters for the homeless, literacy or English-as-a-second-language programs, senior citizen services, to name only a few, would welcome you. They do need for you to make firm commitments so they can depend on you, but most of these kinds of organizations will use your services whenever you can offer them.

Community

Part of the enduring genius of America springs from our willingness to contribute freely to the well-being of all. Nearly every Saturday morning in our town, some group of teenagers has a car wash for one benefit or another. A nearby school conducts an annual flea market to raise money for special community projects. Thousands of moms and dads, brothers and sisters, take up money for the March of Dimes, United Way, and other efforts to raise funds for good causes. This vast reservoir of energy and a willingness to contribute to community and nation make us the great people we are.

I hope you register to vote the day you reach eighteen. It takes only a few minutes to go by the courthouse, city hall, or other voter registration center to have your name entered on the list of qualified voters. It costs you no money to register. You might have to take some proof of age, but voter registration requires no involved process. If you do not know how or where, look in the phone book under local government services and you can secure all the directions you need.

In addition to voting, the community and country need your active participation in the political life of the nation. Who is governor of your state? Congressman from your district, senators from your state? representatives to the state legislature? What kind of political issues effect your community? What national issues have a bearing on the way you and your family live? What kind of information did you pick up from the front page of the daily newspaper? Did you watch even a small portion of the television news last night or this morning? Someone has well said, "We get the kind of government we want." If "We, the People" show little concern about who runs the government and what kind of programs they conduct, we get sloppy administration. If, on the other hand, elected officials and career government employees know that the people have their eyes open, the community and country can anticipate justice, integrity, and effectiveness.

Some of you will have to decide to become public officials. Eventually you will take your seats on school boards, county commissions, zoning authorities, state legislatures, or the US Congress. Take the time now to school yourself in the way our government works. Become a member of a political party. You might be pleasantly surprised to see how eagerly the local office of the political party of your choice would welcome you as a member and volunteer worker.

Young men have to register with the United States Selective
Service when they become eighteen. In most instances, you have
only to go by the local Post Office and fill out a form. You do not
have a choice in such matters, but rather than regard the registration as some kind of harsh duty, sign up with a pride. No one
wants to fight a war, but if the time were to come, you would have
helped in the total effort just by registering.

If possible, give blood to the Red Cross or another certified
blood bank. I have endured a health condition that has always
precluded my donating blood, but my husband and sons have
each donated. The high school from which my husband graduated had a tradition that the seniors gave a pint of blood to the
local Red Cross just before graduation. As your health permits,
make blood donation a habit. Your thoughtfulness in giving
blood just might save someone's life.

You can make a unique contribution as you join efforts to
protect the environment. After all, we only have one Planet
Earth. We've done more to upset nature's fine balance in this
century than in all previous ages of human history combined.
Carelessness, uncontrolled development, too much waste dump-
ing, and inattention to water and air quality can have devastating
long-term effects. The Bible urges us to take care of the earth,
to exercise stewardship, and to manage responsibly the resources
given to us by God and this wonderful planet. Sometimes we
might get the idea that environmentalists all wear grubby tennis
shoes and march up and down the street carrying placards trying
to save an endangered species of the tsetse fly. As a matter of fact,
the conservationist movement in American has frequently turned
the tide away from the destruction of a valuable part of our world.

As you select your ways for contributing, especially outside
your home, tune into your own interests. You will not do a good
job if you work on projects that hold little interest for you. What
do you like to do? What kind of hobbies do you enjoy? If you had
your "druthers," what would you do? Isolate some of those feelings and then match them with your opportunities.

Believe it or not, you cannot save the whole world. You *can* make a difference. Unless, however, you become governor or president, you probably will have an impact on only a piece of the world. Invest your time and efforts carefully so you can have the greatest effect. Most of us face two temptations as we try to decide what kind of contributions to make. We see so much to do that, in our frustration, we do nothing, or we attempt too much with minimal results. Strike a balance. Make some choices. Make an investment. But do not undertake so much that you get frustrated and wind up spinning your wheels.

You will not be the only person out there doing something for God and country. You will have company, maybe not enough, and you may well have to work quite hard to make a dent on a given problem, but if you will look around, you will see some others just as concerned as you.

Avoid looking down your nose at those whom you help as you become involved in working with the poor and deprived. Even the person at the bottom of the social or economic barrel has pride and feelings. Appreciate that person as a human being, the object of God's love and, therefore, worthy of your highest respect.

Don't let yourself feel smug because you are "doing something" while others in your age group are out playing. You can make a difference without becoming snobbish, arrogant, or self-righteous. The world will respect your efforts much more if you will avoid a goody-two-shoes attitude. Thank God and our system of government for the ability and freedom to plunge into problems or situations where you can make a difference. In short, in Jesus' name, give that cup of cold water. Break the "me generation" syndrome.

6

Freedom to Perpetuate

You and I have the freedom to cast our influence far into the future, to perpetuate the gifts and abilities with which we have been endowed. At best, most of us do not live too long. God's plan is that we enjoy the benefits of life, then pass from the earthly scene to live with Him. Personally, I gain special comfort from realizing that in life, or beyond, I am in the hands of God.

Among the senses which God has placed within us is the desire to extend ourselves beyond the days of our own lives. That desire to perpetuate ourselves accounts for such great monuments as the pyramids; noble works of art, such as Michelangelo's *David*; magnificent buildings like the US Capitol; and writings of the quality of King David's twenty-third Psalm, Homer's *Odyessy*, Dante's *Inferno*, Melville's *Moby Dick*, and Hugo's *Les Misérables*.

I think it helps to understand that we did not get *here* by ourselves. Not only did our natural parents conceive and give us life but also a culture, a great civilization, helped bring us to this point in our lives. In America we enjoy the blessings of centuries of Western civilization. We enjoy personal, political, and religious freedom because countless Americans before us risked all they had to create the United States and its way of life.

What we think and do, the way we function daily, has its roots in the past. The past does not hold us in bondage, but we certainly do owe a great deal to people who have lived before us whose names and faces mean nothing to us. As Christians and as Americans, we hold this present time as a trust. You and I have the responsibility to take care of what we have, to contribute to today, as we discussed in the previous chapter. But growing out of our commitment to take care of our families, churches, and country, we have an obligation to make life better for those who come after us.

"Why should I worry about the future? I won't be around to enjoy it or to suffer in it," some of you may say.

Just as you received such a wonderful country from unnamed people from the past so must we determine to do our very best to ensure that future generations of Americans can enjoy life as we do, maybe even more completely.

OK. I want to perpetuate my life and influence. How? Do I have to go out an build a pyramid?

Maybe, but probably not.

Deepen your own faith in God. Spend time with the Lord in studying His Word. As you are riding around in the car alone, sometimes try turning off the radio and thinking about your life; try to figure out what God is up to in you. What kind of plans do you believe He has for you? To deepen your relationship with God is an important way to find the resources to cast your witness into the future.

Recently a friend of mine spent time in a retirement home leading a weekly Bible study. The residents sat in chairs, some in heartbreaking physical condition. Some even had to be propped up in rolling chairs in order to attend the discussion. Naturally, some of these folk felt rather useless because their diminished physical abilities, all too often, made them dependent on others for essential help.

In the course of the Bible study, the teacher looked around the room at the people, many of whom she had known for years. She could feel the frustration, the sense of uselessness that bothered these grand old people. "How many of you have ever taught children at church, in school, or just around the house?"

Nearly all raised their hands.

One lady spoke up and said, "I never had any children of my

own, but I worked with them at church for fifty-five years. Does that count?"

With tears darting to her eyes the teacher said, "I would say yes, that certainly counts."

That elderly woman, experiencing poor health in her late years had not only made a contribution in the then and now, she had perpetuated herself; she had cast her influence into a future that would last beyond her own lifetime.

You say, "Fine, when I am in a retirement home, I will think about perpetuating myself. For now, though, I just want to go to college, get a good job, and have some fun. I'll even give some blood every now and then if that'll make you feel better. But concern myself about perpetuating myself at this stage of my life? You've got to be kidding."

Among the many stirring monuments in Washington, DC, the Vietnam Veterans Memorial, the Vietnam "Wall" as it is commonly known, attracts the most visitors and has the greatest emotional impact on those who view it. The wall is actually a 450-foot-long black granite slab partially buried in the ground. The names of approximately 57,000 men and women who died in Vietnam stare out from the stark wall. Day and night people from around the world walk down the gentle slope that leads to the center of the slab and then back up again, solemnly looking at the names etched in the granite. Families, youth groups, and even foreign visitors can be cavorting, laughing, or picknicking on the Washington Mall. Once, however, they get into the precincts of the memorial, a hush falls over them.

Most visitors simply file past the wall, gazing at the endless lists of names. Others turn to the directory of the order of the listings to find the names of sons, daughters, fathers, brothers, sisters, and friends who died in that conflict.

The memorial came about because some young people who had fought in the war grew sufficiently grieved over the lack of national recognition of their fallen comrades. Jan Scruggs from Bowie, Maryland, a Washington, DC, suburb, enlisted in the army right out of high school. He fought in the war as a *teenager*. He was severely wounded in battle and came out of the army as a specialist fourth class. He dreamed of the memorial and set about to find others who would assist.

He found an ally in the person of Tom Carhart. Tom, somewhat older than Jan, a graduate of West Point, had distinguished himself as an officer in Vietnam. While serving in the war, he saw scores of his former classmates die in the conflict. He was wounded twice.

These young men, and thousands more, also suffered mentally and emotionally because of the mixed feelings many Americans had about the war.

Jan Scruggs, still in his early twenties, began to push and pull to get a memorial built in Washington. Finally he persuaded Congress, the National Park Service, and other officials to allow a memorial to be built on the Washington Mall; but the government, in keeping with its policy, would not pay for the construction. Scruggs and his colleagues would have to raise the money from private sources.

Since the memorial committee could not decide on the type of monument they wanted, they agreed to turn the final selection over to a jury of experts. At this point, I want you to meet Maya Ying Lin. This young woman, an Asian-American, studied architecture at Yale University. At age twenty-two, she submitted a design for the memorial. Out of the thousands of entries, the experts selected hers. They had no idea who had submitted the design, but to the jury, her wall concept for the memorial gathered up the national feelings about the war.

Jan Scruggs, Tom Carhart, and Maya Ying Lin, along with thousands of other young people, have perpetuated themselves. By reaching beyond their own life and time, by being willing to exert energy and act with courage, they have cast their shadows into the unborn future.

You have the grand freedom to gather up the best of your own heritage, refine it, reshape it, then pass it on to your children and grandchildren when they come along.

How?

Get some perspective on your own life and history. Unfortunately many Americans have so little understanding of the past that they have little notion of future directions we should take. By doing some reading in American history you can get a clearer fix on our past. Even reading good historical novels will be helpful. With a bit of history under your belt, you can figure out where you want to go and where you want the country to go.

How many of you have read the Declaration of Independence, the United States Constitution, or any of the other founding documents? You can read the Declaration of Independence in just a few minutes. The Constitution has only a little over 5,000 words, hardly a big volume. When I stand before these documents at the National Archives in Washington, I never cease to marvel that such simple words on yellowed paper have framed this great land of ours. When I stand there, I link arms with the past while feeling myself reaching into the future to Americans not yet on the scene. That sense of past and future, history and transcendence, can help you extend yourself into the future.

Develop some of your own rituals: Fourth of July celebrations, Christmas events, and family reunions. For instance, our family, living in the nation's capital, makes a special effort to join the thousands on the Washington Mall for the Fourth of July celebration. During the day various rock and folk groups give concerts to the two hundred thousand who normally show up. At dusk, the National Symphony gives a rousing patriotic concert on the West Front of the US Capitol. Then, when the sky is fully dark, we all cheer to a spectacular fireworks display against the backdrop of the tall Washington Monument. I never fail to get chill bumps at such a time, even though the weather is sweltering. My family and I are part of something larger than ourselves. That "larger than life" aspect was here before we came. It will be here when we have long passed from the scene.

Another way to link past with the future is to listen to family stories. Every family has scores of stories about Great-Granddaddy and the Civil War, Aunt Janie crossing the desert in a covered wagon, or Cousin Sam making a fortune and losing it all in the Florida Bust. Those stories provide a splendid way for families to know where they came from and give a virtual treasure trove of legends to cast into the future. Of course, you will become part of the folk lore as you live out your own life with all its ups and downs. Listen to family stories. Tell your own stories. Cast yourself into the future, perpetuate the best of who you are.

7

Freedom to Begin Again

Sitting on the lawn in front of the elegant Governor's Palace one summer's night at Colonial Williamsburg, I watched fireworks explode high in the darkness, turning the sky red, green blue, and white. I listened to the music of the bagpipes, the drum and fife corp, and a military band. This festive occasion marked the signing of the Williamsburg Charter, reminding us of our religious freedom as Americans. Life seemed good. Time rolled back while a patriotic glow swelled in each of us as we participated in the celebration.

Walking back to the lodge at midnight, looking up and down the nearly deserted streets of that quaint little city frozen in time, I couldn't help but notice how beautiful, perfect, and neatly laid out the village appeared, especially at that hour of the night. I remarked how uncomplicated life seemed in eighteenth century Williamsburg compared to our time in the twentieth century.

The dignified historian, professor at the University of Virginia who strolled with me, paused for moment, then said, "That's true. Williamsburg does look uncomplicated tonight. But it was not true for the people who started this place. They probably had lots of fears and anxieties." And then as he continued his walk on the brick road, he mused, with a twinkle, "You know there probably were lots of horses and buggies on this road. It could have been pretty messy."

We all laughed as his observation restored a measure of reality to our soaring imaginations.

So true! Life does have its messy side. All is not pleasant. I wish for you the energy and ability to reach forward for the best of life. But more than likely, each of you will crash into some messy reality, sooner or later.

When that encounter does occur, deal with the problem. Do not be afraid to express your hurt, grief, even terror. But hang on to your optimism, your vision for the present and for the future.

You see, young graduate, God gives us the ability to begin again. Peter, impetuous, accident-prone disciple of Jesus, angry and scared nearly witless that night in the garden of Gethsemene, cut off the guard's ear. Peter probably aimed for the man's head, missed and whacked off an ear. You will, no doubt, experience that kind of failure yourself.

Jesus, with a bit of bemusement, in the midst of his greatest crisis, put the ear back on the guard's head. Jesus told Peter to put away the sword. Maybe under His breath, Jesus also told His frightened disciple, "Keep your temper under control. Don't go around taking wild swings in the dark." Unfortunately Jesus does not always put the "ear" back on, but He does give us a chance to begin again.

He forgives our blunders. Only rarely do we make mistakes that ruin our lives forever. Certainly we can make terrific messes and create problems that can take years to correct, but praise be to God, and don't ever forget it, you can begin again.

A student from another country, whose story of escape and survival from a repressive government would rival any best-selling espionage story, crumpled in despair. He had struggled heroically to get himself and some of his brothers and sisters to America. After some fits and starts in American high schools, he had come down to the last days before graduation without enough credits to go through the ceremony. His grades were weak, and his pride was strong.

The school administration should certainly understand why he, who had faced death, did not regularly attend the basic classes with those "children." I knew, also, that his homelife was quite difficult. I knew that he worked as much as he could to help his struggling immigrant family make it. No matter. For all those reasons, he had not passed his classes and could not graduate.

The idea of attending summer school, again with more children, threw the prideful young man into an orbit of rage. The very thought of going to adult school for several weeks likewise deeply offended him. Through his terribly wounded pride he said, "I never thought my life would be like this. I am not supposed to be *here* at this age. I do not want to have to live at home any longer. I do not want to attend school this summer. I cannot let myself do this. I do not know what I will do." His own sense of failure, his pride, and his cultural background collided, nearly paralyzing him.

Life can get terribly complicated. We can wake up one day to find ourselves where we do not want to be. It hurts not to reach the expectations you had for yourself, to miss an important target, to crash into failure. How do you manage such painful situations?

Stop and face reality. Do not waste much time assessing blame. You can learn some lessons from the past mistakes, but don't spend much time wallowing in what might have been.

Look at the remaining pieces. How bad is the situation? What are your options? Assess the problem, the options, and the pieces you have.

Then, make a plan of action. Get help from some dependable people. Then make a move. Do something. You will discover that life can begin again. The freedom to begin again is God's gift to you. Claim that gift. Go for it!

You can take steps toward freedom all your life. You have graduated not to a station in life but to a journey. In every stage of your life, you can find new freedom just as you will never stop encountering boundaries.

Paul sang great songs of his freedom in Christ while, paradoxically, celebrating his joyful bondage to Jesus Christ. With Paul, in Christ we find the freedom to pursue our dreams. He makes us free to try and fail. He grants us freedom to change, to walk away from one set of circumstances to pursue another. He gives us the courage to take a good look at ourselves. He gives us courage to unlock the chains that keep us from true freedom.

You have made an important step, one of the most important in your life. But you have only just begun. Take your steps toward freedom with confidence and an abiding faith in God and yourself.

Where to? What next? You and the Lord can decide and manage. My prayer for you is that you will finish your course with your torch still burning. Maybe some words from Ben Maddox can help us conclude this way:

Growing Older; Growing Wiser

Seems like yesterday, a life ago, a breath;
  Pain, and childlike laughter flow with ease;
  Souls are unburdened and fresh.
    Growing older.

We shut our eyes and life flutters by;
  daytime traumas of each other, never seen, lessen the
  severity, soften their blow.
    Growing wiser.

Learning, living; life is good,
  but anguish is our loneliness, and misty is the
  innocence of long-ago childhood.
    Growing older.

But emotion is what's built in the investments we
  make in one another,
  the depth we feel, the understanding of oneness in
  friends, family, brothers.
    Growing wiser.

Actions separate, and feelings rarely shimmer,
   but the heart holds true the care we have
   as blood and hair grow thinner.
     Growing older.

To laugh tomorrow at the yoke we bear today,
   shines a light glowing dimly at the door of the
   tunnels, far at bay.
     Growing wiser,
     Growing older,
     Growing wiser.

Cyclical is the time we have, swirling dervish
   that we have.
   Stop. Feel it. The hurt means we care; we are
     alive.
   We thrive and falter,
   We flourish and we wither;
   Only God knows the answers we search in vain to
     gather.
Live, feel, touch, experience, only in the mesh of darkness
   and light will we know.
     Growing older.
     Growing wiser.

—A nineteen-year-old
5/27/87   12:40 AM

PS: The brave, young immigrant now has a high school diploma tacked on his wall. Summer school with "children" was not too great a price to pay to earn his first set of keys to freedom.